END-TIME 101

A Wesleyan View
of Prophecy in Progress

Gary Cutler

Copyright © 2024 by Gary L Cutler.

All right reserved.

ISBN 978-1-7331637-2-9

Rapture Revival Ministries
Box 95
Sheridan, IN 46069

Paperback copies of this book
are available on Amazon.

CONTENTS

Introduction: *Why Question the Familiar End-Time?* 1

Chapter One: *Classic Darbyism Logically Imploded* 5

Chapter Two: *The Christ of Daniel's Seventieth Week* ... 11

Chapter Three: *The Rapture Conflict Re-imagined* 25

Chapter Four: *The Time-Transcendent Seventieth Week* ... 49

Chapter Five: *Apocalyptic Time Frames Unsealed* 65

Chapter Six: *A New Historical View of Prophecy* 73

Chapter Seven: *The Biblical Timeline to Armageddon* .. 85

Conclusion: *Moral Realism: A Mindset Awakening* 91

INTRODUCTION
Why Question the Familiar End-time?

Are you ready to embark on a journey of discovery and enlightenment? Are you prepared to question everything you might have thought about the second coming of Jesus Christ? If so, let us introduce you to an alternative perspective that challenges the familiar Scofield Darbyism interpretation. That school of biblical interpretation was developed over the past 150 years by two influential figures, John Nelson Darby and Cyrus Scofield. Perhaps you've never heard of them. Please take a moment to Google their names and discover their impact on biblical interpretation. While we won't delve into their biographies in this book, we invite you to explore their teachings and consider the possibilities of a new perspective on the second coming of Jesus Christ. Our primary focus here is not the individuals behind the teaching but the learning itself. You might resonate with the following diagram of classic Scofield Darbyism, which we'll discuss in detail in this book.

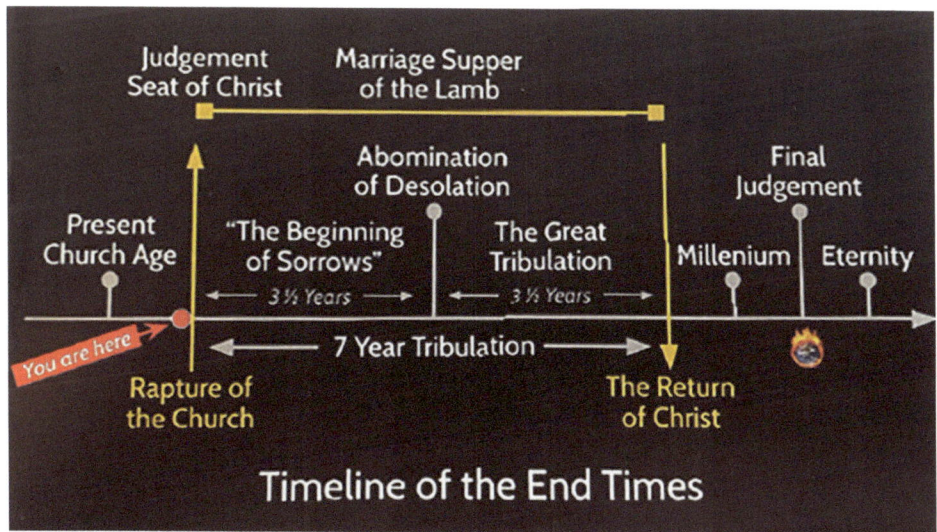

The above time-line of future events is a contemporary illustration of what has been in print and vogue for many years. To begin our analysis of classic Scofield Darbyism, we start with a simple rectangular shape with a line through the center, like this:

The rectangle before you represents a critical time frame called Daniel's seventieth week. Universally believed to be a literal seven-year period, this time frame symbolizes the coming great tribulation. It's a period that's supposed to witness every crucial event of end-time prophecy. But there's one caveat—nothing commences until after the church is first raptured. This theory is of utmost importance, and understanding it will help you comprehend the end times better.

So, without further ado . . .

Are You Ready to Dive In?

The critical razor-like focus that we hammer repeatedly is that Scofield Darbyism is logically based on a particular novel theory of interpreting Daniel's prophecy of the seventy weeks invented by a nineteenth-century Englishman named Sir Robert Anderson. Again, it is not our purpose here to provide the biography of Sir Robert Anderson, so if you are unfamiliar with this historical individual, you are invited to Google the name for basic information about him.

The practice of deriving preconceptions solely from Sir Robert Anderson's interpretation of the seventy weeks and imposing them on the rest of the Bible as a filter is a common practice in popular dispensational teaching. However, this approach ignores the diversity of biblical texts and risks skewing the interpretation of end-time prophecy. Instead, we must approach the Scripture with an open mind, free from any preconceived notions, and interpret it in light of its context and the overall message it conveys. Only then can we hope to gain a deeper understanding of the prophetic messages contained within the Bible.

Discover the fascinating difference between the Wesleyan perspective on end-time Bible prophecy and the classic Scofield Darbyism through John Wesley's interpretation of Daniel's prophecy of the seventy weeks. This interpretation is in stark contrast to Sir Robert Anderson's novel nineteenth-century solution. With our structural analysis and comprehensive diagrams, your imagination will be captivated. Don't let this opportunity to gain a deeper understanding of this intriguing topic pass you by. Join us now.

Reorganizing the End-time the Bible Way

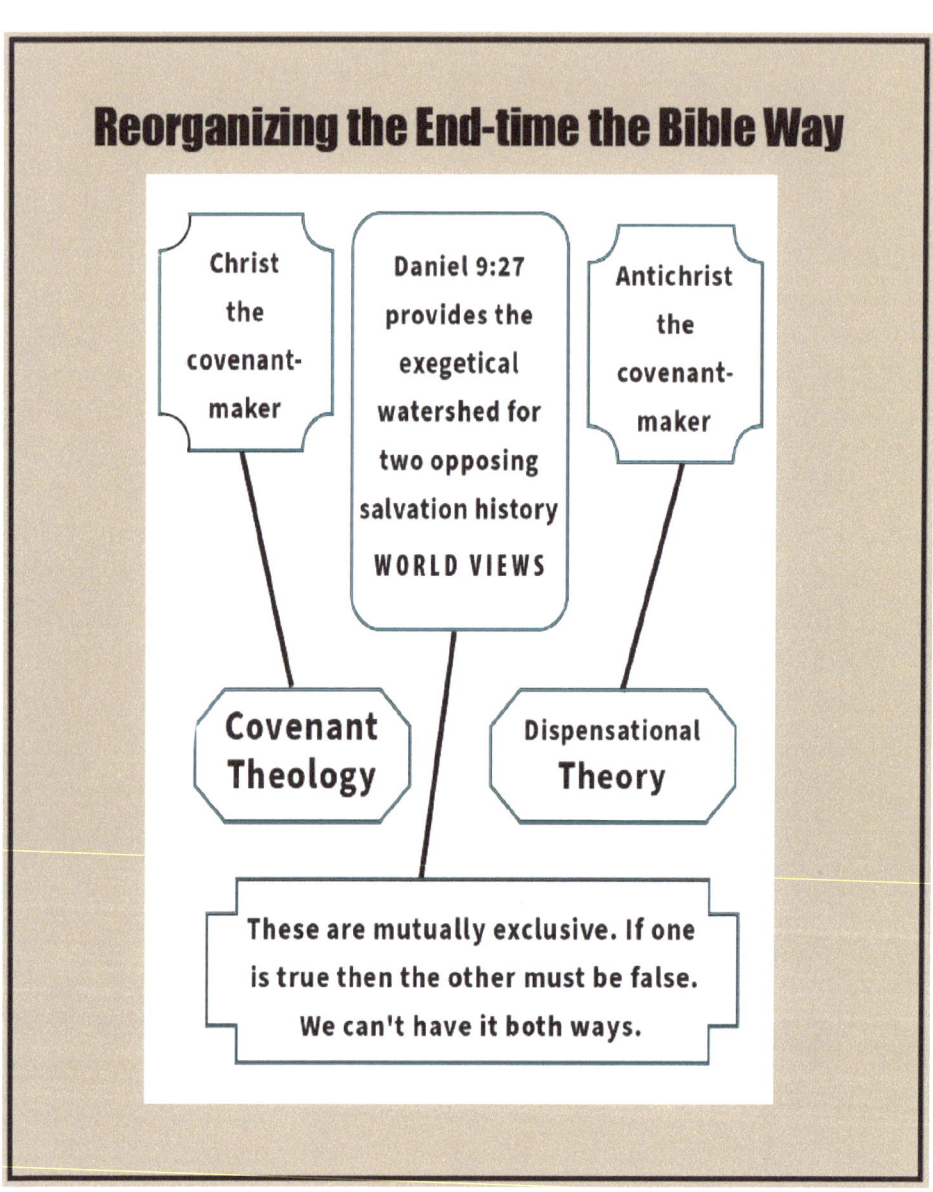

CHAPTER ONE

Classic Scofield Darbyism Logically Imploded

Most contemporary end-time Bible prophecy teachers believe in Scofield Darby's second coming and often refer to Daniel's prophecy of the seventy weeks as the basis for their core ideas. They use the popular preconception of a future seven-year great tribulation period, supposedly derived from Daniel 9:27, as a framework for their end-time scenario. However, there is no mention of any future seven-year great tribulation period in the New Testament. So, how do dispensationalists know that the church is supposed to be raptured out before the beginning of this period? It's time to re-think Daniel's prophecy of the seventy weeks. Here is the full King James Version of that passage.

24. Seventy weeks are determined upon thy people and upon thy holy city, to finish the transgression, and to make an end of sins, and to make reconciliation for iniquity, and to bring in everlasting righteousness, and to seal up the vision and prophecy, and to anoint the most Holy.

25. Know therefore and understand, that from the going forth of the commandment to restore and build Jerusalem unto the Messiah the Prince shall be seven weeks, and threescore and two weeks: the street shall be built again, and the wall, even in troubled times.

26. And after threescore and two weeks shall Messiah be cut off, but not for himself: and the people of the prince that shall come shall destroy the city and the sanctuary, and the end thereof shall be with a flood, and unto the end of the war desolations are determined.

27. And he shall confirm the covenant with many for one week: amid the week, he shall cause the sacrifice and the oblation to cease, and for the over spreading of abominations, he shall make it desolate even until the consummation and that determined shall be poured upon the desolate.

In the prophecy of the seventy weeks by Daniel, the word prince holds great significance. It is mentioned twice, first in verse twenty-five as Messiah the Prince and secondly in verse twenty-six as the people of the prince that shall come shall destroy the city and the sanctuary. The term prince used in both these verses is the same in Hebrew and is referred to as nagid in *Strong's Concordance*, with a reference number of #5057. The word means a leader or ruler, who is also an anointed prince.[1]

The book of Daniel has been interpreted in various ways by scholars, and there is a lot of debate about the identity of the nagid (prince) mentioned in this text. While the nagid in verse twenty-five is undoubtedly the Messiah, some have speculated that the nagid in verse twenty-six is the Antichrist. However, this idea lacks a rational basis and ignores the fact that the same word, nagid, is used for both verses. Therefore, it is logical to conclude that the nagid mentioned in both verses is unequivocally the Messiah. To understand the prophecy's true meaning, it is crucial to reject the notion of the Antichrist and affirm that the nagid in both verses is the Messiah.

Dispensational interpreters argue that there is a difference between the Messiah mentioned in verse twenty-five and the Antichrist that they believe is referenced in verses twenty-six and seven. However, this claim is not correct. It is based on the assumption that verse twenty-five's first nagid (Prince) starts with a capital letter in English, while verse twenty-six's second nagid (prince) does not. But, there is no such distinction in the original Hebrew text. Therefore, this attempted differentiation has no real merit. In reality, the King James translation reflects the dual roles the Messiah was to play rather than two separate individuals. The anointed ruler in both verses refers to the same Messiah, who was despised and rejected (Isaiah 53:3), pierced (Zechariah 12:10), cut off (Isaiah 53:8 and Daniel 9:26), and abhorred (Isaiah 49:7). The difference in the English translation is a

---

[1] Edward J. Young, *The Prophecy of Daniel* [Grand Rapids: WM. B. Eerdmans, 1949], p. 203.

veiled prediction of how the messiah would be revealed when he came —not as royalty, but as the suffering servant mentioned in Isaiah's prophecies.

> O that thou hadst hearkened to my commandments! Then had thy peace been as a river and thy righteousness as the waves of the sea (Isaiah 48:18). O Israel, thou hast destroyed thyself; but in me is thine help (Hosea 13:9).

When we compare the yearning lament of the Father over the estranged relationship between himself and the backslid nation, as expressed in the verses above, with the teaching of Jesus in Matthew 21:33-44, 23:34-39, Mark 12:1-11, and Luke 20:9-18, the meaning becomes clear. Daniel 9:26 is intimating that it was the coming Messiah himself, and not a foreign ruler, who would bring judgment on the messiah-rejecting Jews of 70 A.D. by use of the third-party Roman armies of Titus.

The precedent is well set that in Old Testament times God often used Gentile nations as third-party agencies to punish Israel for her sins. Examples of this can be found in Leviticus 26:18-39; Judges 2:1-15; 3:7-8; 4:1-2; 6:1; 10:6-7; 13:10; II Kings 21:10-14; II Chronicles 28:1-5; 33:10-11; 36:15-21; Nehemiah 9:26-30; Jeremiah 9:11-16; 25:8-14; and 50:17-20. The concept of God utilizing an external force to execute his judgment on his rebellious people is a vital factor in identifying the second nagid of Daniel 9:26. As John 1:11 states, this prince is the one who will come and be spurned by his people, the Jews themselves, who are responsible for their own destruction because they would not have their Messiah to rule over them. Understanding this crucial principle will help us gain a deeper insight into the meaning of this text.

Edward J. Young, a prominent conservative scholar of the Old Testament, examines Anderson's attempt to identify a future figure known as the Antichrist as the covenant-maker of the seventieth week. This attempt is based on the idea that a supposed Roman ruler mentioned in Daniel 9:26 foreshadows an Antichrist figure who is yet to come. However, Young points out the logical absurdity of this theory, given that it is based on an unsupported assumption.

> How can the Roman armies of Titus possibly be regarded as belonging to a prince who has not even yet appeared? This interpretation can be adopted only because of extreme exegetical necessity . . . the emphasis in vs. 26 is not upon a prince from the people, but upon the people who belong to the prince. This prince, therefore, must rule over these people, who can genuinely say that they are his. In other words, he must be their contemporary, alive when they are alive. We cannot, by any stretch of the imagination, legitimately call the army of George Washington, the army of a general, and by that general, have reference to Eisenhower. The armies of Washington are in no sense Eisenhower's armies. And the fact that Eisenhower was born in America many years after the time of Washington's armies does not in the least permit us to say that they are his armies. The people who destroyed the city and the prince that should come (if should come is future, it is future from the standpoint of Dan., not of the destroying people) are contemporaries. Otherwise, the language makes no sense. And if the prince is a contemporary of his people, then the antecedent of 'he shall cause to prevail' [i.e., the covenant-maker of verse 27] cannot be some prince other than that mention in vs. 26 [i.e., the Messiah].[2]

The above considerations effectively shut the door to Anderson's much-vaunted nineteenth-century fiction that some coming Roman ruler—presumably Titus—of 70 A.D. somehow foreshadows an end-time Antichrist figure in Daniel 9:26 and that this Antichrist figure, in turn, becomes the antecedent of the 'he' that is the covenant-maker of Daniel's seventieth week. Nothing suggests that a foreshadowing argument should be inserted in verse twenty-six, as the consistency

---

[2] Young, *The Prophecy of Daniel*, pp. 211-212. Please note that text in brackets is ours, not the original author's.

of dispensational thought requires. The appeal to foreshadowing is a complete fabrication—a smokescreen, if you will—that dispensationalists use to hide the raw speculation being done here. Nothing is plain about the disconnections of logic that dispensational interpreters use, who leap from a presumed Roman ruler of 70 A.D. to a yet future—two-thousand years later, no less!—Antichrist personality, whom they then claim becomes the covenant-maker in verse twenty-seven.

The very idea that anything in the text of Daniel 9:26 foreshadows anything else is simply a figment of the dispensational interpreter's fruitful imagination, the nuance of a deceiving subtlety that cannot be rationally verified in the text. Thus, as we have penetratingly shown, the dispensational beginning premise is grounded in unverifiable obscurity that masks the thought flow of the passage and is just blowing smoke. The question is moot; the bluff called; the cover blown; game over.

Our above-calibrated use of precise language in technical argumentation works. The academic fraud and interpretative hoax perpetrated by Anderson regarding the non-mentioned Antichrist supposed in Daniel 9:26-27 has caused a massive distortion in the worldviews of people regarding end times prophecy. However, a revolutionary truth has come to light—the nagid of Daniel 9:26 is the same person as the nagid of Daniel 9:25, referred to as the Messiah. The Messiah predicted in both verses is the natural and logical antecedent of the 'he' mentioned in verse twenty-seven, who confirms the covenant with many. John Wesley was also of the same opinion. This enlightening truth opens up a radically different version of apocalyptic interpretation called the truth of Christ's return. Let us embrace this truth and look forward to the glorious return of our Savior.

Break-thru Bible Prophecy

Taking knowledge of the end-time to a higher level

FOLLOW THE LOGIC

Wesleyan Bible Propecy

Dispensational Theory

It's all about Daniel 9:27

CHAPTER TWO

The Christ of Daniel's Seventieth Week

Scriptural proofs that Jesus Christ is the divinely-intended covenant-maker of Daniel's seventieth week are abundant and clear. Throughout the Old Testament, we find closely linked to the mission of the promised messiah, the task of promulgating a covenant to the people of Israel. Examples of this are found in Isaiah 42:6; 49:8; 55:3-4; 59:20-21; 61:8-11; Jeremiah 31:31-34; Zechariah 9:11; and Malachi 2:6-7; 3:1.

Notice that the Hebrew word translated confirm in our English text of Daniel 9:27 does not mean making or cutting a covenant. If such were the intended idea, then the ordinary Hebrew idiom for cutting a new kind of covenant (karat brit) should have been used. Instead, the word here means the causing of a covenant that already exists to prevail (literally meaning "to make strong").[1] Promises for a new covenant, such as Jeremiah 31:31-34, lived in the Old Testament. According to Romans 15:8, Jesus Christ made those promises effective or caused them to prevail. This he did specifically through the mediator and revelatory roles that he fulfilled in the totality of his earthly manifestation, as we will see more fully in a moment.

Notice further that it is with the many that the covenant is promised to prevail: "he shall confirm the covenant with many for one week" (Daniel 9:27). And who are these many? Fuller divine revelation gives us no uncertain answer. "By his knowledge shall my righteous servant justify many; for he shall bear their iniquities" (Isaiah 53:11). "This is my blood of the new covenant, which is shed for many for the remission of sins" (Matthew 26:28). "For the promise is unto you, and to your children, and to all that are afar off,

---

[1] Albert Barnes, *Notes on Daniel* [Grand Rapids: Baker Books, 1996], p. 181.

even as many as the Lord our God shall call" (Acts 2:39). "Now I say that Jesus Christ was a minister of the circumcision for the truth of God, to confirm the promises made unto the fathers: And that the Gentiles might glorify God for his mercy; as it is written, For this cause I will confess to thee among the Gentiles, and sing unto thy name. And again he saith, Rejoice, ye Gentiles with his people. And again, Praise the Lord all ye Gentiles; and laud him, all ye people. And again, Isaiah says, There shall be a root of Jesse, and he that shall rise to reign over the Gentiles; in him shall the Gentiles trust" (Romans 15:8-12 and Acts 15:7-17). From this correlation of texts, it becomes apparent that Daniel 9:27 foresaw both Jews and Gentiles being included in the promises of the new covenant. Though the weeks' prophecy was to the Jews and about the Jews, it was not exclusively for the Jews. Verse twenty-four is too encompassing for that.

In contrast to this Spirit-directed way of harmonizing Scripture, the amazing craftiness of the dispensational system can be seen by the patch-quilt manner in which the architects of this theory linked together an array of surface-related proof texts individually wrested from their surrounding contexts. For example, dispensationalists claim an Antichrist identification of the covenant-maker in Daniel 9:27 based on its supposed harmony with Isaiah 28:15-18, Ezekiel 21:25-27, Daniel 8:25, 11:21-45, and John 5:43. However, a careful study of these texts within the confines of their respective contexts reveals that their supposed harmony with an alleged covenant-confirming activity of Antichrist in Daniel 9:27 is more apparent than real.

Using the entire body of Old Testament messianic revelation as our background the following points can be made. In the appearance of Jesus of Nazareth God had remembered his holy covenant (Luke 1:68-70), that is, the covenant of promise that was confirmed before of God in Christ four-hundred thirty years before the giving of the law of Moses (Galatians 3:17). As a minister of the circumcision for the truth of God, Christ came to confirm the promises made unto the fathers (Romans 15:8—an obvious allusion to Daniel 9:27) and is thereby plainly declared to be not only the messenger (Malachi 3:1) but also the mediator of the new covenant (Matthew 26:27-28; Romans 11:27; Galatians 4:24-31; I Timothy 2:15; Hebrews 8:6; 9:15; 10:16, 29; 12:24; and 13:20-21). According to John Wesley, Christ confirmed the new covenant of Daniel 9:27 in six ways: "He shall confirm. Christ established the new covenant: (1) By the testimony of angels, of John the Baptist, of the wise men, of the saints then living, of Moses and Elijah. (2) By his preaching. (3) By signs and wonders. (4) By his holy life. (5) By his resurrection and ascension. (6) By his death and blood-shedding."[2] Following Wesley's well-known gospel paradigm of Christ revealed as the believer's prophet, priest, and king, we now proceed to explain how Jesus Christ caused the Christian revelation of the new covenant to prevail in Daniel 9:27.

Christ as Prophet

First, we observe that the Christian gospel story begins in the Old Testament, as early in our Bibles as Genesis 3:15. In this text, God promised Eve that her seed, though initially being bruised by the serpent, would ultimately crush the serpent's head. That promised seed of the woman is Christ. Christ is also the promised seed of Abraham, and the one to whom the blessing promised to all nations in Genesis 12:1-7 is now being fulfilled (Romans 4:13-17; II Corinthians 1:20; and Galatians 3:16-29).

Throughout the history of Israel, God revealed himself to his people through individuals known as prophets. The first prophet chosen by God was Moses, as mentioned in Deuteronomy 34:10 and Hosea 11:13. On Mount Sinai, Moses received the Ten Commandments and other laws that were meant to govern the covenant relationship between God and the Israelites, as well as their relationship with one another (Exodus 19:5-6). As the law-giver, Moses became the spiritual

---
[2] John Wesley, *Commentary on the Bible*, p. 369.

authority over Israel. In Deuteronomy 18:15-18, God promised to send another prophet like Moses, whom the Israelites would be required to follow. According to Acts 3:23-24, Jesus fulfilled this promise God made to Israel in Deuteronomy 18:15-18 in the following ways.

1. Many of his own countrymen recognized him as a prophet. See, for example, Matthew 16:14; 21:11, 46; Mark 6:15; 8:28; Luke 7:16, 39; 9:8, 19; 24:19; John 4:19; 6:14; 7:40, 52; and 9:17.

2. He exercised prophetic authority as a Spirit-anointed spokesman for God. Examples are Matthew 7:28-29; 21:23-27; Mark 1:22, 27; 11:27-33; Luke 4:36; 20:1-8; John 5:26-27; and 6:63, 68.

3. He fulfilled the prophetic role of calling the nation in repentance back to God. See for example Matthew 4:17; 9:13; 11:20; Mark 1:14-15; 2:17; Luke 5:32; 10:13; 11:32; 13:3, 5; and 15:7.

4. Like Moses, Jesus taught the precepts of God's rule among men. For example, see Matthew chapters five through seven and thirteen; also 18:23-35; 20:1-16; 22:2-14; Luke 13:20-21; 18:16-25; John 3:3, 5; and 18:36.

5. Like Moses, Jesus established a new law, creating a new covenant with God. Examples include John 13:34-35, Romans 5:18, Galatians 4:24-28, 1 Timothy 2:5, and Hebrews 8:6.

As the prophet greater than Moses, Jesus taught that true righteousness consists of loving submission of heart to the absolute kingship of God. The Old Testament required this understanding of holiness and promised the experience (Matthew 22:37, 40; Deuteronomy 6:4-5; and Leviticus 19:18). The same thought is seen by comparing Matthew 5:48, 6:22-32, 23:26, Mark 7:21-23, and Luke 6:45 with Deuteronomy 30:6, Jeremiah 32:39, and Ezekiel 36:25-27.

In his public ministry among the Jews two-thousand years ago, Jesus fulfilled the prophetic role of teacher, giving to fallen humanity the full and final revelation of the nature and will of God (John 1:18). God is holy and requires that we be holy to enter heaven (Hebrews 12:14). Since Jesus, too, is God (John 1:1 and 10:30), holiness is now attainable through submission to Christ's authority as one with the Father. To receive eternal life, all must obey Jesus Christ, who is the gatekeeper of the highway of holiness. There is no other way to heaven except through him (John 10:9; 14:6 and Acts 4:12).

Christ as Priest

Jesus fulfilled the role of the prophet during his public teaching ministry on earth two-thousand years ago. He also, by his atoning death on the cross of Calvary, fulfilled the role of priest. The function of the priests in Old Testament times was to serve as the intermediary between God and man. This was accomplished by the offering of appropriate sacrifices for sin. God required such sacrifices due to man's fall from original holiness at the dawn of history. We read this in Genesis chapter three and Hebrews 9:22, where we note that God himself offered the first blood sacrifice in the Garden of Eden (Genesis 3:21).

In the early history of Israel, God made special promises concerning two priests. The first was Melchisedec, king of Salem, and the second was Phinehas, the grandson of Aaron. The account of Melchisedec is found in Genesis 14:18-20. God promised to send Israel a future priest-king with endless life after the order of Melchizedek (Psalm 110:4; Zechariah 6:12-13; Hebrews 5:5-10; 6:20; and 7:11, 21). God also promised Phinehas's descendants an everlasting covenant of peace (Exodus 40:15; I Samuel 2:35; I Chronicles 9:20; Psalm 106:30-31; Jeremiah 33:15-26; and Malachi 2:4-8 and 3:1-3). The New Testament declares that these promises concerning Melchisedic and Phinehas, both for an eternal priesthood and for an everlasting covenant of peace, were fulfilled in the saving work of Jesus Christ. Here is how that fulfillment has now been realized in Christ:

1. Jesus' priestly atonement work is revealed as the primary purpose for his incarnation (Matthew 20:28; Mark 10:45; Luke 9:56; 19:10; John 1:29; 5:51; 10:11, 15, 17-18; and I John 3:4, 8).

2. He withdrew his offer of the new covenant of peace from the nation that rejected him and offered it instead to his disciples (Luke 19:41-42; John 1:11-12; 14:27; 16:33; and Exodus 24:7-11).

3. He ratified this new covenant of peace with his disciples by instituting a new sacrament symbolizing the significance of his impending death (Matthew 26:26-28; Mark 14:22-25; Luke 22:17-20; John 6:51-58; and Exodus 24:7-11).

4. Christ's death on the cross of Calvary is declared to be the meritorious grounds upon which new covenant promises for pardon, peace, and purity are realized (Romans 3:24-26; 5:1, 11; Ephesians 2:13-18; Colossians 1:20-22; and Hebrew 9:13-15).

The simplicity of the gospel is that Christ died for our sins according to the Scriptures (I Corinthians 15:3). As our great high priest, Jesus paid the ransom price for our redemption (I Peter 3:18 and Romans 5:8). As a result of his one sacrifice for sins forever, salvation and eternal life are now offered as the gift of God's grace (Ephesians 2:8-9). According to the Bible, salvation is from sin to true holiness of heart and life. This includes justification and regeneration, or beginning sanctification, as well as entire sanctification. Justification happens by the two-fold obedience of repentance and water baptism; regeneration occurs by the baptism of the Holy Spirit that subsequently follows.[1] This is seen in the Pentecostal salvation paradigm presented in John 3:5; Acts: 2:38; Titus 3:4-7; and many other places.

---

[1] The difference between justification and regeneration can be stated more clearly as follows: Justification refers to the imputation of Christ's righteousness to the believer for the remission of his past sins only (Romans 3:24-26). On the other hand, regeneration involves the initial inner cleansing that is accomplished by the infilling of the Holy Spirit, which enables the believer to keep God's commands and leads to the beginning of a holy life (Acts 15:8-9).

Christ as King

Jesus fulfilled not only the Old Testament mediator roles of prophet and priest, but also the role of king. In Old Testament Israel, a king's function was to deliver, protect, guide, and prosper God's people. Remarkable promises were made to Israel's second and greatest king, King David. These promises, also known as the Davidic Covenant, are documented in II Samuel 7:7-14; 23:5; I Kings 2:4; I Chronicles 17:2-27; Psalm 89:3-4, 34-37; 132:11-12; and Jeremiah 33:15-17 and 25-26. Here is how these promises were fulfilled in the historical event of Jesus Christ.

1. Jesus was a literal physical descendant of King David (Matthew 1:17 and Romans 1:3).

2. He was born king of the Jews (Luke 1:31-33 and Matthew 2:2).

3. His most significant concern in his public ministry was for the kingdom (see Matthew 4:23; 9:35; and other passages too numerous to mention; in summary, the word kingdom is used one-hundred thirteen times in the four gospels alone).

4. Jesus died being publicly acknowledged as king of the Jews (Matthew 27:11, 37; Luke 23:3, 38; and John 19:19-22).

While the preceding observations are important, God's promise to David found its fullest realization in the resurrection, ascension, and present seating of Christ on the right hand of the Father in heaven. The core of the Christian revelation is the idea that God raised Christ to sit on old King David's promised everlasting messianic kingdom throne at the time of Jesus' resurrection and ascension two-thousand years ago. Here is the breakdown of the New Testament facts:

1. Christ began his kingdom reign at the time of his ascension to the Father in 30 A.D. (Psalm 2:6-7; Acts 13:22-23, 32-34; Hebrews 1:3-5; Psalm 110:1; Luke 20:41-44; Acts 2:30-36; Hebrews 1:1; 10:12-13; Daniel 7:13-14; Luke 24:51; Acts 1:10-11; Psalm 68:18; and Ephesians 4:8-10).

2. Jesus now reigns in total harmony with the biblical messianic ideal. (Matthew 28:18; Ephesians 1:22; Colossians 3:1; Hebrews 8:1; and I Peter 3:22). He is the stone that the builders rejected that was made the chief cornerstone of the Christian church (Psalm 118:22; Ephesians 2:20; and I Peter 2:7), and the stone upon the heavenly throne John saw in Revelation 4:2-3.

3. Jesus will continue to reign until the end of the age when he will deliver his messianic kingdom of salvation to the Father (Luke 1:32-33; Acts 3:21; I Corinthians 15:24-28; and Hebrews 1:8, 13).

Whatever accrued dominion Satan may have gained over fallen humanity in pre-Christian ages has now been annihilated through the power of Christ's death and resurrection (John 12:31; Ephesians 4:8; Colossians 2:15; II Timothy 1:10; and Hebrews 2:14-15), so that believers through the abundance of gospel grace may now have complete triumph over the devil (Romans 16:20; I Corinthians 2:14; James 4:7; I John 4:4; 5:4, 18; and Revelation 12:11). Thus, it is not necessary to circumvent or truncate the power of the gospel in this present age by assuming, as dispensationalism does, that Christ must return to earth again to bind the devil, for as Vic Reasoner, in his book *The Hope of the Gospel: An Introduction to Wesleyan Eschatology*, has well pointed out: "he has authorized his church to do just that!"[1] Satan flees from the person who resists him (James 4:7). How is this possible unless his power is now broken by the one that is stronger than he (Matthew 12:24-30; Luke 11:21-22; and I John 4:4)?

John Wesley believed that Christianity is the final dispensation from God, and there will be no other after it. He maintained that any claimed revelations of a more superior age than Christianity are the work of Satan.[2] Wesley's view was that dispensational teaching, which postpones the establishment of the kingdom until the second coming of Jesus to set it up during the millennial reign, fails to understand the messianic nature and content of New Testament Christianity. Such

---

[1] Vic Reasoner, *The Hope of the Gospel: An Introduction to Wesleyan Eschatology*, p. 61.
[2] *The Works of John Wesley*, vol. 5, p. 314.

teaching is based on the hope of a messiah yet to be, but it does not align with the revealed Christ of the New Testament. Sir Robert Anderson, a nineteenth-century co-founder and patriarch of the dispensational theory, demonstrated an inability to see Jesus Christ confirming a covenant in the New Testament.[1] This reflects a significant blindness enveloping those who are infatuated with their misguided preconceptions and prejudices.

Despite the opinions of men, two thousand years ago, the primary purpose of Christ on earth was to confirm a covenant, the entire body of New Testament Christian revelation. This renowned New Testament scholar, Herman Ridderbos, agrees when he writes that "The entire gospel of the kingdom [which Christ preached] can be explained in the categories of the covenant promised by God"—a gospel presented in the New Testament as a message, a gift, and a power.[2]

Christ in All the Seventy Weeks

Daniel's prophecy of the seventy weeks is all about Jesus Christ. He appears in this prophecy in the following three ways: First, the time of Messiah's birth is announced in verse twenty-five: "Know therefore and understand, that from the going forth of the commandment to restore and to build Jerusalem unto Messiah the Prince shall be seven weeks, and threescore and two weeks." Second, Messiah's substitutionary, sacrificial death is foretold in verse twenty-six: "And after threescore and two weeks shall Messiah be cut off, but not for himself." Third, his enduring accomplishment is highlighted in verse twenty-seven: "And he shall confirm the covenant with many for one week, and amid the week he shall cause the sacrifice and the oblation to cease, and for the overspreading of abominations he shall make it desolate, even until the consummation."

---

[1] Sir Robert Anderson, *The Coming Prince*, p. 54.
[2] Herman Ridderbos, *The Coming of the Kingdom* (Phillipsburg, NJ: Presbyterian and Reformed Publishing Company, 1962), pp. 201 and 76.

From Cyrus to Bethlehem:
The True Chronology
of the First Sixty-Nine Weeks Unveiled

The most natural place to begin the chronology of Daniel's seventy weeks is 538 B.C. when the new Persian King Cyrus issued his famous proclamation allowing the Jews to return to Palestine following the seventy years of the Babylonian Captivity. Cyrus' proclamation is recorded in II Chronicles 36:22-23 and Ezra 1:1-4. The prophet Isaiah nearly a century and a half earlier, had mentioned Cyrus by name as the one who would cause the city of Jerusalem and the temple to be rebuilt (Isaiah 44:28 and 45:13). In response to Cyrus' proclamation, about fifty-thousand Jews led by Sheshbazzar left Babylon for Jerusalem in the year 536 B.C.

According to Daniel 9:25, sixty-nine weeks were to elapse between the enabling proclamation of Cyrus and the appearing of the Messiah: "Know therefore and understand, that from the going forth of the commandment to restore and to build Jerusalem unto Messiah the Prince shall be seven weeks, and threescore and two weeks." The Hebrew word for weeks in this prophecy is sevens, which scholars understand to be a period of seven years. These weeks also refer to prophetic years of three-hundred sixty days each, not our Gregorian solar calendar years of 365.2422 days each. Thus, the seven weeks refer to a period that is forty-eight solar years long (49 prophetic years x 360 = 17,640 days ÷ 365.2422 = 48.3 solar years, rounded back to 48 years). Likewise, the sixty-two weeks refer to a period that is four-hundred twenty-eight solar years long (62 weeks x 7 years = 434 prophetic years x 360 = 156,240 days ÷ 365.2422 = 427.8 solar years, rounded up to 428 years).

The first seven weeks period was the time especially given to reconstruction: "the street shall be built again, and the wall, even in troubled times" (Daniel 9:25). First, the street, then the wall, were to be constructed in that order. The street included the city and the temple; the wall represented both the city's physical and spiritual defenses. The first part of this dual reconstruction era, the street period, or the time allotted for the rebuilding of the city and temple, lasted from the start of the project at the command of Cyrus in 538 B.C. until the new temple was completed and dedicated on March 12, 515 B.C.[1] This was twenty-three solar years (538 B.C. - 515 B.C. = 23 years).

The second part of this dual reconstruction era, the wall period, or the time allotted for rebuilding the city's physical and spiritual defenses, began with Ezra's journey to Jerusalem in 458 B.C., as recorded in Ezra 7:6-10. It continued until the covenant renewal had fully implemented national reform in 433 B.C. (see Nehemiah chapters nine and ten). We can calculate the year 433 B.C. by understanding that the revival of the covenant occurred twelve years after Persian King Artaxerxes I Longimanus permitted Nehemiah to repair the walls of Jerusalem in 445 B.C. (see Nehemiah 2:6, 5:14, and 13:6). The date 445 B.C. minus twelve years equals 433 B.C. This second reconstruction period involving Jerusalem's physical and spiritual defenses lasted twenty-five solar years (458 B.C. - 433 B.C. = 25 years).

The sixty-two week period began where the seven weeks reconstruction era ended, at the covenant renewal in 433 B.C. These sixty-two prophetic weeks (after the conversion to our solar calendar has been made as we saw above) are thus four-hundred twenty-eight solar years instead of four-hundred thirty-four years long. Four hundred and twenty-eight solar years subtracted from 433 B.C. brings us to 5 B.C. as the most likely year of the birth of Jesus of Nazareth the Messiah (433 B.C. - 428 years = 5 B.C.).[2]

---

[1] Jack Finegan, *Light From the Ancient Past* [Princeton, 1948], p. 196.

[2] See Appendix Four of *The Century of the New Testament* by E. M. Blaiklock for the merits of dating the nativity of Jesus in the year 5 B.C.

The Chronology of the 69 Weeks

The 1st **seven week** period is the time allotted for reconstruction 7 times 7 equals 49 prophetic years or 17,640 total days		The **62 week** period is the intervening inter-testament era
The **street** building period--a total of 8,320 days	The **wall** building period--a total of 9,320 days	62 times 7 equals 434 prophetic years or 156,240 total days extending from October 4, 433 B.C. to the birth of Christ on July 13, 5 B.C.
Extending from the proclamation of Cyrus on May 31, 538 B.C. to the dedication of the new temple March 12, 515 B.C.	Extending from the departure of Ezra for Jerusalem on March 28, 458 B.C. to the renewal of the covenant October 3, 433 B.C.	Thus exactly fulfilling the total 69 weeks between the proclamation of Cyrus and the appearance of the Messiah as per Daniel 9:25
Recorded in Ezra 1-6	Recorded in Ezra 7-10 & Nehemiah	

(Originally published in *Is the Great Tribulation in Daniel 9:27?* by Gary L. Cutler, © 1992)

Scholars agree that King Herod the Great died in the spring of 4 B.C. So the birth of Jesus Christ had to have occurred before King Herod's death, for it was Herod who sought to kill Jesus after the visit of the wise men from the East. He did slaughter the children in Bethlehem and its environs up to two years old based on the calculation of the first appearance of the guiding star as the magi had related it to him (Matthew 2:7).

Here are three reasons why our solution to the chronology of the sixty-nine weeks is much better than Sir Robert Anderson's previously acclaimed theory, as described in his book *The Coming Prince*.

1. We begin the weeks at the monarchy of Cyrus, which academic integrity requires.[1] SRA, by contrast, begins the weeks with the travel permission granted by Artaxerxes I Longimanus to Nehemiah in March-April 445 B.C.

---

[1] John Calvin, *Commentary on the Book of Daniel*, vol. 2, p. 213.

2. We have identified a precise division between the seven-week and the sixty-two-week periods, which SRA did not. This division is necessary for the precision methodology. Later, dispensational authorities realized this logical weakness and proposed that the division was indicated by the end of prophecy with Malachi. However, the question remains as to the exact day on which Malachi's prophecy ended.

3. According to biblical scholarship, the dates assigned to events in the life of Christ are in agreement with our conclusions. SRA, by contrast, places the end of the sixty-nine weeks at the Triumphal Entry in the year 32 A.D.[2] However, scholars agree that the crucifixion most likely occurred in the year 30 A.D. Joachim Jeremias proves from astronomy that the year 32 A.D. cannot be considered as a possibility for the date of the crucifixion.[3]

Sir Robert Anderson's theory of interpreting the seventy weeks was mistaken in the correct identification of the covenant-maker of verse twenty-seven and the chronology of the first sixty-nine weeks. Our penetrating exposure of the academic flaws in SRA's theory spells the rational overthrow of the whole dispensational system of biblical interpretation. It's all misguided from A to Z.

This fact is of profound significance due to the overwhelming influence of popular dispensational teaching on the evangelical masses in America today. Yes, indeed, now is the time for contemporary dispensational endgame prophecy experts to pony up, stop presuming, and start proving the exegetical legitimacy of their foundational assumptions. They often refer to Sir Robert Anderson's theory when pressed academically, but this theory is now permanently debunked by the sure guns of careful analysis provided in this book. It is a proven intellectual hoax and an academic fraud, we repeat, that supports a modern religious cult promoting a gospel that differs from the one presented in the New Testament. This needs to be addressed and corrected.

---

[2] *The Coming Prince*, p. 127.
[3] *The Eucharistic Words of Jesus* [London: SCM Press, student ed., 1961], p. 41.

Prophetic Studies in Contrast

CLASSIC DARBYISM

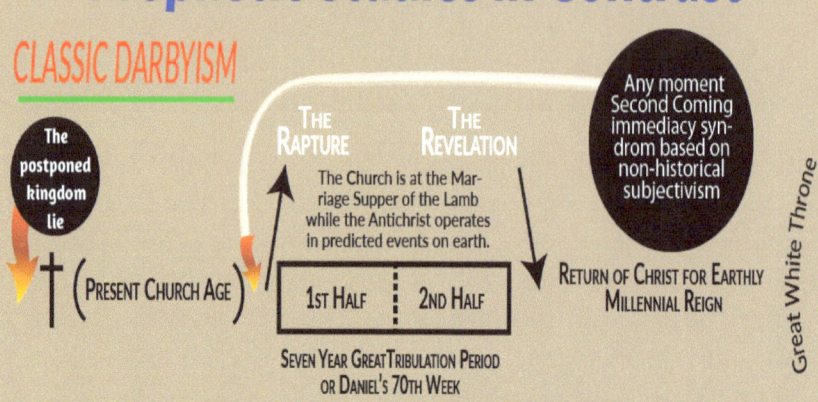

THE WESLEYAN CREATIVE END-TIME BIBLE PROPHECY ALTERNATIVE

The above popular theory of end-time fiction is based on 19th Century Sir Robert Anderson's misguided interpretation of Daniel's prophecy of the 70 Weeks. John Wesley believed, by contrast, that Christ, not Antichrist, is the divinely-intended covenant-maker of Daniel 9:27. Wesley believed that the covenant of the 70th week was the "new covenant" of the whole Christian revelation. This plays out into an entirely different view of salvation history that can be presented as follows:

- The kingdom set up on the Day of Pentecost
- Daniel's 70th week is an apocalyptic symbol for the whole present Christian messianic kingdom age of redemption--the last dispensation of the Holy Spirit.
- The kingdom delivered up at the Last Judgment when Christ returns

CHAPTER THREE
The Rapture Conflict Re-imagined

It's time to break free from the limitations of Sir Robert Anderson's theory of the seventy weeks. We cannot continue to accept the assumptions that have been derived from it, such as the speculative future seven years, the Antichrist's covenant-making and breaking activities as a placeholder, and the idea that Christ intended to establish a political, nationalistic Jewish kingdom during his first coming, which is currently on hold. We must open our minds to new possibilities and reconsider these misnomers that have been holding us back.

Jesus' Rapture Teaching

Jesus provided clear teachings about the timing of the rapture. In John 6:39-40, 44 and 54, he stated that the resurrection of believers occurs on the last day four times. Therefore, we must understand what he meant by last day. The plain literal meaning of these words suggests that there can be no rapture before the last day. Here is what a few of the best authorities in Greek and theology say the expression last day means in John 6:39-40, 44, 54; 11:24 and 12:48.

> *Bauer, Arndt, & Gingrich, A Greek English Lexicon of the New Testament and Other Early Christian Literature*: " . . . last day (of this age) (p. 347) . . . . of time least, last, coming last or at the last of something that is left . . . (the last)" (p. 314).
>
> *Thayer's Greek English Lexicon of the New Testament*: "it refers to the last day of the present dispensation when Christ shall return to earth for the final judgment (p. 253). . . . the last day of the present age, the day in which Christ will return from heaven, raise the dead, hold the final judgment, and perfect his kingdom" (p. 278).

Hastings Bible Dictionary: ". . . it refers to the last day of the present dispensation when Christ shall return to earth for the final judgment" (vol. 1, p. 573).

Kittell's Theological Dictionary of the New Testament: "It brings temporal being in the present eon to an end is thus the last day" (vol. 11, p. 953).

Barnes' Notes on the New Testament: ". . . the day of judgment" (p. 247).

Whedon Bible Commentary: "The Day that closes the series of human history and inaugurates the final judgment" (p. 288).

Pulpit Bible Commentary: " . . . the final consummation of his redemptive work . . . . The final resurrection and final judgment" (p. 262).

Based on the evidence presented, it seems clear that some popular speculative end-time prophecy teachers are not being honest when they suggest that the phrase last day in John 6:39-40, 44 and 54 can be interpreted to mean any random time, allowing them to inject the idea of a rapture at any moment. However, Jesus specifically stated that he would resurrect believers on the last day, not at any time before that. It is important to understand the intended meaning of this passage and not to be misled by those who twist its meaning to fit their own agenda.

According to Jesus, the resurrection of believers on the last day is just one aspect of the general resurrection of the dead. This is made clear in John 5:28-29, where he states that "the hour is coming, in which all that are in the graves shall hear his voice, And they shall come forth; they that have done good unto the resurrection of life; and they that have done evil, unto the resurrection of damnation." It's important to note that there is only one hour for this event to occur. Furthermore, this single, general resurrection event will lead to two eternal destinations. All will hear his voice and come forth to either the resurrection of life (Luke 14:14) or the resurrection of damnation (Matthew 12:36-37), depending on whether they have done good or evil, respectively (verse twenty-nine).

Some teachers speculate that because certain passages in the Bible, such as I Corinthians 15:51-52 and I Thessalonians 4:16-17 only mention the resurrection of the righteous dead, the resurrection of the wicked dead is necessarily excluded from happening at the same time. However, the lack of explicitly stating the inclusiveness of the resurrection in every instance is not a logical or exegetical proof against the biblical teaching of a general resurrection of the dead, as taught in John 5:28-29.

Jesus unequivocally taught that the general resurrection event mentioned in John 5:28-29 will directly merge into the universal judgment of all humanity when he returns. This is affirmed in Matthew 16:27, which states that "the Son of man shall come in the glory of his Father with his angels, and then he shall reward every man according to his works." Similarly, in Matthew 25:31-46, it is written that "When the Son of man shall come in his glory and all the holy angels with him, then shall he sit upon the throne of his glory: and before him shall be gathered all nations: and he shall separate them one from another as a shepherd divides his sheep from the goats."

When it comes to the rapture, there's a significant difference between what Jesus taught in Matthew 25:31-46 and what many end-time prophecy experts suggest. Specifically, these experts often refer to Matthew 25:31-46 as evidence of a judgment of Gentile nations to determine their eligibility for the millennial kingdom based on how they treated the Jews during the tribulation period. However, Jesus himself made it clear that immediately after the universal judgment that happens at his second coming, the people on his left will go to everlasting punishment, while the righteous will enter eternal life (Matthew 25:46). It's important to note that Jesus did not mention anything about a one-thousand-year Jewish kingdom being established on earth after his return. This interpretation is flawed because it insists that Jesus' brethren in Matthew 25:40 refers exclusively to racial Jews. Instead, Jesus identified his real brethren as his disciples (Matthew 12:47-50 and 28:10), which includes the entire sanctified Christian church (Hebrews

2:11-12). Therefore, it's critical to follow Jesus' teachings and understand that our actions and beliefs will be judged based on our relationship with him, not on our treatment of any particular group of people. Let us do our best to live according to his teachings so that we may enter eternal life and avoid everlasting punishment.

Jesus described the universal judgment scene that happens at his second coming as the harvest of the kingdom age. Matthew 13:24-30, 38-43, 47-50.

> Another parable put he forth unto them, saying, The kingdom of heaven is likened unto a man which sowed good seed in his field: But while men slept, his enemy came and sowed tares among the wheat, and went his way. But the tares appeared when the blade was sprung up and brought forth fruit. So the servants of the householder came and said unto him, Sir, didst not thou sow good seed in thy field? From whence then hath it tares? he said unto them, An enemy hath done this. The servants said unto him, Wilt thou then that we go and gather them up? But he said, Nay; lest while ye gather up the tares, ye root up also the wheat with them. Let both grow together until the harvest: and in the time of harvest I will say to the reapers, Gather ye together first the tares, and bind them in bundles to burn them: but gather the wheat into my barn. . . . he answered and said unto them, he that sows the good seed is the Son of man; The field is the world; the good seed are the children of the kingdom, but the tares are the children of the wicked one; The enemy that sowed them is the devil; the harvest is the end of the world; and the reapers are the angels. Therefore, as the tares are gathered and burned in the fire, so shall it be in the end of this world. The Son of man shall send forth his angels, and they shall gather out of his kingdom all things that offend, and them which do iniquity, And shall cast them into a furnace of fire: there shall be wailing and gnashing of teeth. Then shall the righteous shine forth as the sun in the kingdom of their Father. Who hath ears to hear, let him hear . . . . Again, the kingdom of heaven is like unto a net that was cast into the sea

and gathered of every kind: Which, when it was full, they drew to shore, and sat down and gathered the good into vessels, but cast the bad away. So shall it be at the end of the world: the angels shall come forth, sever the wicked from among the just, cast them into the furnace of fire: there shall be wailing and gnashing of teeth.

The book of Matthew does not mention a Jewish millennial reign between Christ's second coming and the end-time harvest judgment. Despite this, some end-time prophecy teachers ignore Christ's clear doctrine about his messianic kingdom in Matthew thirteen and try to impose their post-second coming Jewish millennial reign theory upon the New Testament. They distinguish between a mystery form of the kingdom of heaven and a future Jewish millennial reign associated with the kingdom of God expression. However, it is clear from a comparison of Matthew 4:17 with Mark 1:14-15, Matthew 11:11 with Luke 7:28, Matthew 13:31 with Mark 4:30-31, Matthew 13:33 with Luke 13:20-21, and Matthew 19:14 with Luke 18:16 that the kingdom of heaven and the kingdom of God are the same thing. They both refer to the establishment of Christ's messianic kingdom of redemption on earth at the time of his first advent. Thus, to repeat, there is no basis for the speculative end-time prophecy teachers' claim that there will be a Jewish millennial reign between Christ's second coming and the end-time harvest judgment. It is important to recognize that Christ's kingdom of redemption has already been established on earth, and we should focus on cultivating it instead of speculating about a future Jewish millennial reign. Let us not be misled by false teachings but instead embrace the truth of Christ's message in Matthew thirteen.

In Matthew twenty-four, Jesus does not mention anything about a seven-year period that can be divided into first-half or second-half distinctions, nor does he say anything about Antichrist making or breaking a peace treaty with the Jews. The term Antichrist is never mentioned in this chapter. These notions are simply preconceptions that have been read into this text from the current widespread misinterpretation of Daniel 9:27 and Revelation chapter twenty.

Rather, Matthew twenty-four serves as a forewarning and a description of the destruction of Jerusalem in 70 A.D., as was prophesied in Daniel 9:26-27 and 12:11-12.

In Matthew 24:34, Jesus predicted that the generation of his contemporaries would not pass away until all the prophecies about Israel's destruction mentioned in the Old Testament were fulfilled. He used the parable of the fig tree's budding to compare the signs of Jerusalem's impending destruction with the appearance of buds on a tree. This parable marked the transition from early spring to the long summer growing season that would occur after the event. The destruction of Jerusalem in 70 A.D. was significant, but it was not the second coming of Jesus Christ or the end of all things apocalyptic, as some radical Preterists believe. Instead, it ushered in a new season, the long summer growing season of the worldwide Christian witness. This season will culminate in the fall harvest when Christ returns for the final judgment, as mentioned in Matthew 13:36-43 and 47-49.

Paul's Rapture Teaching

Paul taught that there will be one general, universal, and singular resurrection of the dead in Acts 24:14-15. "But this I confess unto thee, that after the way which they call heresy, so worship I the God of my fathers, believing all things which are written in the law and the prophets: And have hope toward God, which they also allow, that there shall be a resurrection of the dead, both of the just and unjust." It is important to note that the plain, literal sense of language teaches two facts here: (1) There will be a resurrection of the dead—not plural, as in "resurrections of the dead." (Note that the singular form is also used in Acts 23:6 and 25:31). (2) This general resurrection event will include both the just and the unjust.

Paul taught that the general resurrection of the dead, which takes place at Christ's second coming, also issues in the universal judgment of humanity. See Acts 17:30-31; Romans 2:6, 16; 3:6; 14:9;

II Corinthians 5:10; and II Timothy 4:1. In this, Paul agrees with Jesus in Matthew 16:27, 25:31-46, John 12:48, and Revelation 22:12. Paul further taught that the rapture would happen at the sounding of the last trumpet, as stated in I Corinthians 15:51-52. This is similar to Jesus' teaching of the rapture on the last day in John chapter six. In both instances, the word last implies finality, which contradicts the idea of the rapture occurring before anything else.

The pre-tribulation rapture concept requires a specific time frame to make sense. However, I Corinthians chapter fifteen does not mention any end-time tribulation time frame. Therefore, we cannot conclude that Paul is referring to the rapture before a seven-year tribulation period in this passage. The reason people believe that is due to a preconceived theory that provides the time frame without scriptural evidence. The precluded theory behind it all is SRA's misguided interpretation of Daniel's seventieth week, as was dissected previously. Paul teaches that in I Corinthians 15:51-52, the rapture of believers at the last trump's sounding involves the destruction of the last enemy, death. This final victory over death only comes at the end of Christ's present kingdom reign. Let's follow the logic in Paul's timing of the rapture here.

1. The endpoint is marked as the time when Christ delivers up the kingdom to the Father: "Then cometh the end, when he shall have delivered up the kingdom to God, even the Father" (verse twenty-four).

2. Christ's kingdom reign precedes the destruction of the last enemy, death: "For he must reign, till he hath put all enemies under his feet. The last enemy that shall be destroyed is death" (verses twenty five and six).

3. The destruction of the last enemy death is directly associated with the resurrection and rapture of living believers described in verses fifty-one and two: "So when this corruptible shall have put on incorruption, and this mortal shall have put on immortality, then shall be brought to pass the saying that is written, Death is swallowed up in victory" (verse fifty-four).

4. This resurrection/rapture of believers, when the last enemy, death, is swallowed up in glorious victory, thus comes after, not before, Christ's messianic kingdom of redemption reign. "For he must reign till he hath put all enemies under his feet. The last enemy that shall be destroyed is death"—words that can only describe a final resurrection at the end of time.

In I Thessalonians 4:15-17, Paul describes the rapture of believers as a very audible, visible, and public event. He tells us that the Lord himself will descend from heaven with a shout, with the voice of an archangel, and with the trumpet of God. The dead in Christ will rise first, followed by those who are alive and remain, who will be caught up together with them in the clouds to meet the Lord in the air. This is a powerful and awe-inspiring image, but two common errors are made when interpreting this passage. First, some assume that the context here is the seven-year tribulation period, which has been shown to be non-existent. Second, some suggest that the sounds mentioned in verse sixteen should not be taken literally, but only subjectively within the inner consciousness of believers, in order to support the pre-tribulation rapture notion. However, this is not being true to a literal interpretation of the Bible. We should remember that Paul's words were written to encourage believers and provide them with hope in the face of adversity. The idea of being caught up to meet the Lord in the air is a comforting thought for many Christians. However, we must be careful not to impose our own preconceptions on the text. Instead, we should seek to understand it as it was originally intended, and allow it to speak to us in a meaningful way.

The idea that there is a pre-tribulation rapture in the New Testament is speculative, as there is no specific seven year time frame anywhere mentioned. This is much like trying to distinguish between identical twins—we can only tell them apart if we see them together in the same place at the same time. Nowhere in the New Testament can we find the rapture and the revelation, separated by a stated seven year time frame, appearing together in one place simultaneously. This makes it challenging to distinguish them as separate entities and not the same event. As such, we should be cautious when interpreting these passages and not jump to conclusions based on speculation alone.

The dispensationalist distinction between Christ's coming for his saints in the pre-tribulation rapture and his coming with his saints later is not supported by the Thessalonian text, which states that when Jesus comes for the rapture it is with his saints as well (I Thessalonians 3:13 and 4:14). Such distinctions are artificial and based on mere semantics, rather than stated time frames, which are necessary to distinguish between a pre-tribulation rapture and Christ's public revelation. However, these time frames do not exist to prove the dispensational end-time prophecy fantasies.

In II Thessalonians 1:7-10, Paul teaches that the rapture of the church coincides with the time of Christ's revelation. He says that believers will rest when Christ comes to judge the wicked (verse seven), while the wicked will be judged when Christ comes to be glorified in the saints (verses nine and ten). Paul's repetition of the word when emphasizes this correlation between the rapture and the judgment. Therefore, it seems that the rapture cannot be separated from Christ's coming at the revelation, at least not by any discernible amount of time.

In II Thessalonians chapter two, Paul warns that the rapture will only occur after a great apostasy within the Christian movement. This is evident throughout the chapter, particularly in verse four: "The man of lawlessness is revealed sitting in the temple of God." This verse states that lawlessness will gain control of what is supposed to be Christian churches, leading to apostasy. Interestingly, the word temple in verse four is the same Greek word Paul uses to describe the body of Christ, the church, in I Corinthians 6:19. Thus, it is plausible that the restraining force of II Thessalonians 2:6-7 may refer to the pure New Testament faith that resides within the orthodox Christian church (I John 5:4). In the great antinomian apostasy of the latter days this faith is lost (II Thessalonians 2:3; Luke 18:8; I Timothy 4:1-2; II Peter 2:1-4 and Revelation 11:7), and Satan is unleashed (Revelation 9:1-11; 11:7; 17:8 and 20:7). When the apostasy has run its course, the Lord will return for the last judgment (II Thessalonians 2:8 and Daniel 12:7).

The idea that II Thessalonians 2:6-7 refers to the removal of the Holy Spirit during the pre-tribulation rapture is commonly taught but lacks evidence from the text. Nowhere does the Bible mention the removal of the Holy Spirit, and even if he is the restraining force mentioned in verses six and seven, how could his removal prove the occurrence of a rapture? It seems more likely that the absence of the Holy Spirit implies a backslid church that has grieved away the Holy Spirit. This interpretation aligns better with important doctrinal issues related to the ministry of the Holy Spirit. John Wesley's view of the restraining force in II Thessalonians 2:6-7 is pertinent to this discussion. Commenting on verse six, he writes: "That which restraineth—the power of the Roman emperors, when this is taken away the wicked one will be revealed."[1] Many of the church fathers believed that the fall of the Roman Empire was an apocalyptic sign[2] and that the Thessalonians 2:6-7 restrainer concept referred to the apocalyptic fall of Rome based on Daniel 7:11, 26. John Chrysostom (A.D. 347-407), for example, in his "Homilies on Thessalonians," makes this statement:

> Only there is one that restraineth now until he be taken out of the way," that is when the Roman empire is taken out of the way, then he shall come. And naturally. For so long as the fear of this empire lasts, no one will willingly exalt himself, but when that is dissolved, he will attack the anarchy, and endeavor to seize upon the government both of man and God. For as the kingdoms before this was destroyed, for example, that of the Medes by the Babylonians, and that of the Babylonians by the Persians, and that of the Persians by the Macedonians, and

---

[1] *Explanatory Notes Upon the New Testament* [Schmul Reprint, one vol. ed.], p. 535.

[2] Ernest Best, *A Commentary on the First and Second Epistles to the Thessalonians* [New York: Harper & Row Publisher, 1972], p. 296.

that of the Macedonians by the Romans: so will this also by the Antichrist, and he by Christ, and it will no longer withhold. And these things Daniel delivered unto us with all clearness.[1]

Lactantius (A.D. 260-330), in "The Divine Institutes," was another church father who took up a similar strain. He depicted the apocalyptic downfall of the Roman world order in the following vivid language:

> For all the earth will be in a state of tumult; wars will everywhere rage; all nations will be in arms and oppose one another; neighboring states will carry on conflicts with each other, and first of all, Egypt will pay the penalty for her foolish superstitions and will be covered with blood as with a river. Then the sword will traverse the world, mowing down everything and lying low all things as a crop . . . the cause of the desolation and confusion will be this; because the Roman name by which the world is now ruled, will be taken away from the earth, and the government return to Asia, and the East will again bear rule, and the West be reduced to servitude.[2]

Other church fathers distinguishing between Rome and the last anti-Christian protagonist include Barnabas, Tertullian, Pseudo-Ephaream, Commodian, Cyril of Alexander, and Ambroaister. To summarize, Wilhelm Bousset, in his prodigious work on the Antichrist legend, affirms the following:

> None the less is the conception itself a common-place for nearly all the Fathers, beginning with Irenaeus. They hold not that the Roman empire is the Antichrist, but that the Antichrist will appear after its fall. [Rome] . . . so far from being the Antichrist stands in the way of his coming, while he is declared to be a non-Roman ruler.[3]

---

[1] *Library of the Nicene and Post-Nicene Fathers of the Christian Church*, 13:389.

[2] *The Anti-Nicene Fathers*, 7:212.

[3] *The Antichrist Legend: A Chapter in Christian and Jewish Folklore* [London: Hutchinson and Co., 1896], p. 123.

According to Walter K. Price, a dispensational author, the early non-Roman Antichrist tradition was strong.[1] It was only during the Protestant Reformation era that the idea of a Roman Antichrist gained prominence. The Protestant Reformers rightly associated the spiritually degenerate Roman papacy of the sixteenth century with the spirit of antichrist. However, it was Sir Robert Anderson and the nineteenth century futuristic school of dispensational premillennial prophecy teaching that mistakenly linked an individual associated with Rome to an imagined final Antichrist figure based on a wrong interpretation of Daniel 9:27.

Peter's Rapture Teaching

According to Peter, even though Christ comes to believers and reside in them through the Holy Spirit in this present age, his glorified bodily presence must remain in heaven until the restoration of all things at the consummation (Acts 3:19-21). This restoration would include the return of Christ to judge both the living and the dead (Acts 10:42 and I Peter 1:13 and 4:5), and the eternal manifestation of the new heaven and a new earth where righteousness fully reigns (II Peter 3:13). However, before the new heavens and the new earth are fully manifested, the current earth must first be destroyed by fire (II Peter 3:7, 10 and 12). Peter further explains that this destruction of the world by fire will happen suddenly, unexpectedly, and like a thief in the night.

The interpretation of II Peter 3:10 regarding the end times is often misunderstood. Some believe that the verse refers to a secret rapture of the church, but this is not what the text suggests. Instead, it predicts the judgment of the earth by fire, which will come unexpectedly

---

[1] *The Coming Antichrist*, pp. 19-27. According to George Eldon Ladd's book, *The Blessed Hope* (p. 37), the futuristic interpretation of Revelation 6-19 was introduced by a Spanish Jesuit named Ribera in 1590. Ribera's primary goal was to counter the traditional historical interpretation of the book of Revelation held by Protestants, which linked Romanism as a system of the antichrist. Additionally, Ribera is also credited with inventing radical preterism, which argues that the second coming of Christ occurred in 70 A.D., according to R. C. H. Linski's *Commentary on the Book of Revelation* (p. 194).

like a thief in the night, and will be as devastating as the flood in Noah's day.[2] Jesus, Paul, and Peter agree that this judgment will not include a secret rapture of the church but will be a catastrophic retribution for wickedness on earth. Paul had stated in I Thessalonians 5:3 that the day of the Lord would come like a thief in the night, catching those who are clamoring over peace and safety off guard. This does not refer to a so-called first three-and-a-half-year period of false peace under the Antichrist. Instead, Jesus, Paul, and Peter uniformly speak of sudden destruction happening at the end of time, which will be so catastrophic that there will be no possible escape.

It is essential to understand that the end times will not be a time of peace but a time of judgment. The cataclysmic events predicted in the Bible will come unexpectedly, and we must be prepared for them.

John's Rapture Teaching

In Revelation 1:7; 6:12-17 and 11:11-12 John teaches that when Christ returns, every eye will see him. This is in agreement with Jesus' teachings in Matthew 24:30 and Paul's teachings in I Thessalonians 4:16-17. As neither Jesus nor Paul taught about the pre-tribulation rapture of the church, it can be assumed that John did not have that idea in mind either. In fact, John tells us exactly when the rapture will occur. The rapture, which Paul describes in I Corinthians 15:51, John says will occur when the last trumpet sounds in Revelation 11:15-18. This biblical correlation serves as a reminder that God's word is precise and that everything that has been prophesied will ultimately come to pass.

---

[2] D. D. Whedon, a distinguished Wesleyan scholar, presents seven compelling arguments in his *Commentary on the New Testament* (vol. 1, pp. 285-286) that clearly distinguish the destruction of Jerusalem by the Romans in 70 A.D. from the end-of-the-world return of Christ for the last judgment. These arguments draw attention to the contrasting gradual approach of the former and the unexpected materialization of the latter. Whedon's arguments are compelling and should be taken into consideration when examining the differences between the two events.

Re-thinking the Biblical Antichrist Concept

It's time to rethink our understanding of the biblical Antichrist teaching. The fact is that the idea of a pre-seven-year secret rapture of the church is non-existent, and there is no future seven-year concept in the first place. This realization has a significant impact on how we perceive the Antichrist. The traditional belief is that he will be a one-world government ruler who will operate within the context of a seven-year career. However, it's time to challenge this mindset and seek a deeper understanding of the biblical teaching on the Antichrist. Let's open our minds to new possibilities and explore what the Bible truly says on this topic.

Antichrist is mentioned only a few times in the Bible—I John 2:18-19, 22; 4:3 and II John 7. It's interesting to note that John, the author of these verses, is very precise in his definitions. Thus, it's important to pay close attention to what he says and doesn't say about this concept. According to John, there were many antichrists present during the first century A.D. (I John 2:18). This indicates that the Antichrist is not just one person who will emerge at the end of time. John's message is clear—we shouldn't focus solely on one person as many antichrists have already arrived. In fact, the appearance of many antichrists, not just the Antichrist, is a relevant indication of the last days. So, let us keep our eyes open and be mindful of the signs of the end times.

In I John 2:18, John clarifies that the last time is now upon us, not due to the arrival of the Antichrist, but because of the prevalence of many antichrists. It is not evident from the text that John himself believed in a singular Antichrist figure at all. Instead, it is more probable that he is correcting the misconceptions of his readers, who had heard about such a figure from inter-testament non-revelatory sources. John further affirms that these many antichrists do not arise from outside the Christian faith, as many might assume. Rather, they emerge from within the community of believers as apostates who have abandoned their Christian faith (I John 2:19).

The epistles of John provides a clear definition of the Antichrist, stating that anyone who denies that Jesus of Nazareth is the Messiah is considered one. John's definition is precise: "every spirit that confesses not that Jesus Christ comes in the flesh" (I John 4:3 and II John 7). According to John, this is the only description needed to identify the Antichrist. It is a powerful reminder that faith in Jesus as the Christ is essential to our spiritual well-being. Let us always remember John's words and hold fast to our faith in the one true Messiah.

The Mark of the Beast Explained

It is important to clarify that the widespread belief regarding the "mark of the beast" is not entirely accurate. Many assume that this event will take place during a future seven-year tribulation period after the rapture of the church, but this conviction is not supported by the Bible. In fact, the Bible does not mention any specific seven-year end-time prophetic period. Therefore, it is crucial to re-examine this assumption and come to a more informed understanding of what the Bible actually teaches. Let us not be misguided by unfounded beliefs but rather seek truth through careful study of the Scriptures.

The first thing to clarify about the mark of the beast concept in the book of Revelation is to determine the identity of the beast itself. It is commonly believed that the beast refers to a future leader of a one-world government, but this is not accurate. The beast does not represent a single person; rather, it stands for an empire or a whole kingdom. Specifically, it represents the Roman Empire as a whole, not any single, ruler whether in the past or future. We will provide more information on this as we delve further into chapters thirteen and seventeen.

Dispensational interpreters should acknowledge the use of personification in the biblical prophecies. Personification is a literary device that attributes human characteristics to non-human entities. In Daniel chapter seven, verses seventeen and twenty-five, the words king and kingdom are used interchangeably. For instance, the four domains of Babylon, Persia, Greece, and Rome are called four kings. Similarly, Rome is personified as representing a compilation of those earlier three kingdom powers in 2:44, the king of fierce countenance in 8:23-24 (cf. 7:7), and the willful king of 11:36-45 (cf. 7:23). These passages refer to the emergence of Rome as the dominant kingdom power in the latter part of the inter-testament period and have nothing to do with a projected lone Antichrist figure who will only appear thousands of years later. The book of Daniel does not convey the idea of a personal one-world government leader, the Antichrist, who is yet to arise at the end of this present age. Daniel's prophecies relate to the Roman world at Christ's first advent. It is left to the New Testament writers to take us on from there.

In order to understand the mark of the beast passage in Revelation chapter thirteen, we need to first look at the background provided in chapter seventeen of the book of Revelation. This chapter mentions eight kings or kingdoms in verses ten and eleven, which is important to note.

> 10. And there are seven kings, five are fallen, and one is, and the other is not yet come; and when he cometh, he must continue a short space.
>
> 11. And the beast that was, and is not, even he is the eighth, and is of the seven, and goeth into perdition.

The book of Revelation sheds light on Satan's actions throughout history. It mentions seven Gentile kingdoms that opposed God's chosen people, Israel, in the Scriptures. These kingdoms are Egypt, Assyria, Babylon, Persia, and Greece, which have all fallen; Rome, which existed when the book was written; and finally, a future kingdom that will last only for a short while and which we will have occasion to identify in a few minutes. In Revelation 17:11, it is revealed that the eighth king is none other than Satan himself—the mastermind behind all seven empires mentioned in verse ten. John also refers to Satan as "the beast that was and is not, and shall ascend out of the bottomless pit, and go into perdition" in 17:8. Before the first coming of Christ, Satan ruled over the Gentile nations, while God was the king of Israel. But after Christ's victory, Satan's reign is no longer uncontested, as Jesus has been established as Lord of all. It's interesting to note that the description of Satan as the beast ascending out of the bottomless pit is found in multiple places, including Revelation 9:1-11, 11:7, and 20:7-10, as well as chapter seventeen. This means that the Bible considers Satan as a powerful and dangerous adversary who seeks to control the world. As we continue to study Revelation, we will discover more about this theme and understand the importance of remaining faithful to God in the face of evil.

As we delve deeper into the meaning of the mark of the beast, let's turn our attention back to Revelation chapter thirteen. Here, we come across two distinct beast kingdoms, with the first being discussed in verses one through ten and the second in verses eleven through eighteen. By studying these passages closely, we can gain a clearer insight into the significance of the mark of the beast—an understanding that could prove to be invaluable in discerning the true end-times.

In Revelation 13:1-2, Satan is depicted as a dragon who gives his power, authority, and throne to another beast that emerges from the sea. The crowns on Satan's heads, as described in 12:3, are now placed on the horns of this sixth beast empire of 17:10, which represents Rome. These seven heads of the Roman beast signify the collective dominion of the seven heads of the four beast empires outlined in Daniel 7:1-7 and illustrate Rome's universal rule during the New Testament era. The first beast of Daniel 7:4 (Babylon) had one head, the second beast of 7:5 (Media-Persia) had one head, the third beast of 7:6 (Greece or Macedonia) had four heads, and the fourth terrifying-looking beast of

Daniel 7:7 had one head, making the total number of seven heads with ten horns.

Revelation 13:1-2 describes a beast that represents Rome and assimilates the characteristics of the lion, the leopard, and the bear from the previous empires mentioned in Daniel 7:4-6. This beast has seven heads and ten horns which are a manifestation of the power of the previous empires. In verse three, John sees the Roman beast wounded by a sword, with only one of its heads injured. This injured head symbolizes Rome alone, and is prophetic of how the sword of the Spirit injured the pagan beast in the hands of the apostolic church. However, the near-fatal wound was healed, and the pagan beliefs of Rome were revived in the medieval Roman Catholic Church.

In Revelation 13:11, John describes the emergence of a second beast that replaces Rome. Unlike the first beast that came out of the Mediterranean Sea, this new beast has two horns, representing its two-party system of governance, and emerges from a wider land area. Some scholars interpret this second beast as representing the new American Empire, founded in 1776, while the Holy Roman Empire ended with the French Revolution on the other side of the Atlantic in 1791. Revelation 13:5 mentions the duration of the first two-phased Roman beast empire as lasting forty-two months, which is a mysterious time frame that will be clarified later in the book. The book of Revelation warns us of a second beast empire (the seventh king or kingdom of 17:10) that will possess the same authority and power as the first one. Its ultimate objective is to promote the genius of the former Roman beast and encourage the world to worship it. This is a direct threat

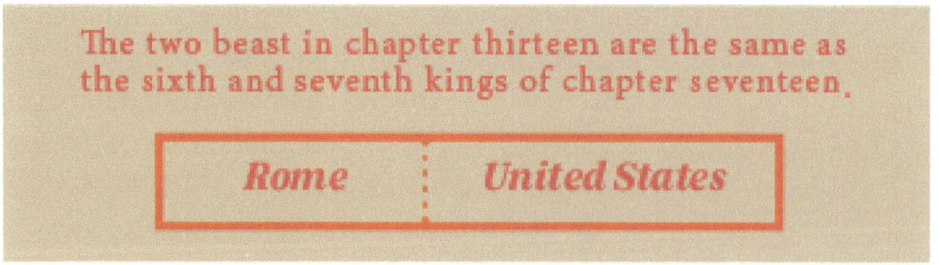

to Christianity, as the mark of the beast represents the expansion of Rome's anti-Christian paganism on a global scale. Let us be vigilant and take a stand against this evil force that seeks to undermine our faith and values.

In the book of Revelation, chapter thirteen, the concept of the mark of the beast refers to the pagan lifestyle that results from the worship of human empires. This concept has been present throughout history, from the first Christian century to the present day. During the first eighteen hundred years of church history, the dominant imperial power was Rome, which sought to impose its mark on the societies under its influence. Today, the world's lone superpower is exerting its imperial dominance as well, and although the names of the empires have changed, the branding remains the same.

The mark of the beast is a symbol of ownership and is usually displayed on either the hand or the forehead. It represents our actions and thoughts respectively. Those who bear this mark are considered to be owned by the empire, and their thoughts and actions reflect this ownership. Those who accept the mark of the beast or the pagan lifestyle tied to ancient Rome live in a way that goes against Christian beliefs and values. They lack a Christian mindset and way of life. As Jesus said, our actions speak louder than words. It is important to understand that in Revelation 13:17, the term "buying and selling" refers to the act of supporting oneself by participating in the local economy. In ancient Rome, where the society was pagan, there was immense pressure for Christians to conform to the pagan lifestyle. Therefore, it is crucial for us to remain steadfast in our faith, resist the empire's influence, and stay true to our Christian beliefs. By doing so, we can bear witness to the world and demonstrate the power of Christ's love and truth.

In apocalyptic symbolism, the number six represents humanity, while the mark of the beast signifies the number of an unsaved person, which is the opposite of Jesus' new creation. Interestingly, the number six is multiplied by three to indicate the trinitarian concept of completeness. Those having the mark of the beast today are those subscribing to the philosophy of humanism, which is in stark contrast to those who have received the seal of the Spirit or the branding of Christ, as portrayed in 3:12, 7:3-4, 14:1 and 22:4. It is crucial that we reflect on our choices and ensure that we align ourselves with the teachings of Christ so that we can be a part of his new creation and receive the seal of the Spirit.

The Fate of the Jews in End-time Prophecy

After dispelling common misconceptions surrounding the concept of the mark of the beast, it's important to discuss a critical issue in the widely accepted end-time teaching of Scofield Darbyism. This concerns the Jewish people and their predicted fate during the supposed seven-year tribulation period. However, we have already established that this time frame is a myth. Therefore, it's time to question the validity of teachings based on such fallacies and demand a rational and evidence-based approach to understanding the end times.

The debate surrounding Sir Robert Anderson's prophetic clock theory concerning the Jews has led to a lot of conflict and confusion among those trying to understand the Bible's actual teachings. Anderson proposed that God's clock paused two-thousand years ago and will resume ticking only after the pre-tribulation rapture. However, many scholars argue that this theory is detrimental to our understanding of the Christian gospel as presented in the New Testament. They suggest that it is a substitute for holiness or antinomianism revived[1] based on a lawless interpretation of the Bible. It is crucial to critically consider these arguments and strive to grasp the Bible's actual teachings. Doing so will enable us to understand God's plan for the world and our place in it.

---

[1] Numerous Wesleyan scholars have written explicitly against the exegetical and theological fallacies of dispensationalism. Please visit our website at *www.rapturerevival.org.* for a wealth of additional information.

Romans Nine Through Eleven

This passage is essential for comprehending God's plan for the Jews. These chapters do an excellent job of outlining the absence of any specific time frames for the Jews' conversion in the future. Also, it is crucial to consider that the New Testament doctrine of Christ's return for the final judgment suggests that no one can be saved after the second coming. The insights provided in this section of Romans are vital for understanding the necessity of accepting Christ before the Judgment Day.

> "And so all Israel shall be saved: as it is written, There shall come out of Sion the deliverer and turn away ungodliness from Jacob" (Romans 11:26).

This verse is often used as a proof text by those who insist that all the Jews, or the Jews as a nation, are guaranteed to get saved sometime in the future, presumably at the end-time. In Romans chapters nine through eleven Paul does not talk about the second coming of Christ or the end of the age. Instead, he discusses the plan of salvation, specifically, how all humanity is equally eligible for salvation. Paul concludes that God has allowed unbelief to both Jews and Gentiles so that he can display his mercy towards them all (Romans 11:32). This mercy is being shown through the gospel, which is a revelation that everyone should respond to equally with obedient faith (II Corinthians 6:2). This whole section of Roman chapters nine through eleven is a closely connected unit of thought, forming a tightly knit argument or thesis.

In this passage, Paul's main argument is that being a Jew does not give anyone an advantage or special privilege in terms of salvation. According to Paul, confessing Jesus as the Savior and Lord is the only way to be saved. Paul emphasizes that there is a faithful Israel, which is different from natural Israel, and that racial identity alone is not enough to be included in the people of God (Romans

9:6-11).² However, Paul also states that Jews can still be included in the people of God if they do not persist in unbelief. Paul's argument here is aimed at the Gentiles. He is urging them not to repeat the same mistake as the Jews by trusting in their self-righteousness (Romans10:1-4) or engaging in antisemitism. Paul warns that Gentile believers should be cautious lest they suffer the same fate of being cut off if they follow the Jews' example of unbelief (Romans 11:18-21). Additionally, the Gentile is not allowed to assume that the Jews' current situation will not change if they accept Jesus (Romans 11:23). They can and will be grafted in again if their attitude towards Jesus changes.

There is no logical reason to assume that Paul had the concept of national Israel or the Jews as a nation in mind in Romans 11:26, or even in Galatians 6:16. Instead, his genuine concern was with the believers in Christ and the possibility of including all his fellow citizens in the number of the elect. Paul already recognized that some of them, including himself, were included in that number even at that time (Romans 11:5). Although the Jews were blinded to some extent (II Corinthians 4:4), he acknowledged, their blindness was never total, but only partial (Romans 11:25). Please note that there is no stark contrast between the nation of Israel's total blindness to the claims of Christ during this present age and their sudden opening of all their eyes to Jesus at the second coming. The partial blindness of the Jews will continue until the fullness of the Gentiles comes in, as Paul states in verse twenty-five. In this context, fullness means all. The Romans 11:25 text is not about the number of elect among the Gentiles but about all the Gentiles.

Paul's point in Romans chapter eleven is that whether the remaining unbelieving Jews give up their unbelief or whether all the

---

² It's crucial to debunk the idea of a racial Jew tracing back to Abraham. The notion is incorrect because Abraham was a Syrian (Deuteronomy 26:5), and all races now trace back to Noah (Acts 17:26). The Jewish identity is based on religion, not race. Abraham didn't establish a new race despite having several sons. Instead, God established a new relationship with him based on a religious covenant. This information is essential to help us correct any misconceptions about the Jewish identity and promote a better understanding of the faith.

Gentiles get saved, it will all happen in the same way.[3] Therefore, Romans 11:26 reads: "And so [literally, in the same way or the same manner] all the true Israel, whether they be Jews or Gentiles, will be saved." And what way is that? It is the way of mercy (11:30-32) found by obedient faith in Christ as Saviour and Lord that Paul had already described in Romans 10:4-13.

The Identity of the Two Witnesses Revealed

Dispensationalists commonly believe that the two witnesses in Revelation chapter eleven are two individual Jewish evangelists who prophesy during either the first or second half of the future seven-year tribulation period. However, this assumption is misguided because the seven year tribulation period itself does not exist. The one-thousand two-hundred sixty days in Revelation 11:3 is not a literal three and a half year period but rather an apocalyptic symbol for the second division of Daniel's seventieth week, depicting the present new covenant age between 70 A.D. and Christ's return for the last judgment. This alternative interpretation will become more apparent as we proceed through this book. For now, we refer to the following simple diagram to help our minds adjust.

---

[3] Everett I. Carver, *When Jesus Again*, gives this explanation of Romans 11:26:

> Thayer states that houtos 'refers to what precedes; in the manner spoken of; in the way described'; as well as 'thus, so.' Now just how was Israel being saved at the time Paul wrote this letter to the Romans? They were being saved in small numbers (Romans 11:14) and they were being saved through the preaching of the gospel (Romans 10:12-16). Therefore, we conclude that Paul is saying that all of Israel that become saved will be saved after this fashion, according to this pattern, or in the manner just described . . . . Those who teach a future conversion of the total Jewish population at the second coming translated houtos as though it were an adverb of time. These render it as though Paul were saying, 'And at that time,' or 'Then all Israel will be saved.' But this interpretation is not justified. Had that been Paul's meaning, surely he would have used tote, an adverb of time. Had he done that, he would have meant that at some future time all of Israel would be saved. But houtos does not say that, and it is improper and misleading to attempt to force such an interpretation of what Paul did not write (pp. 198-199).

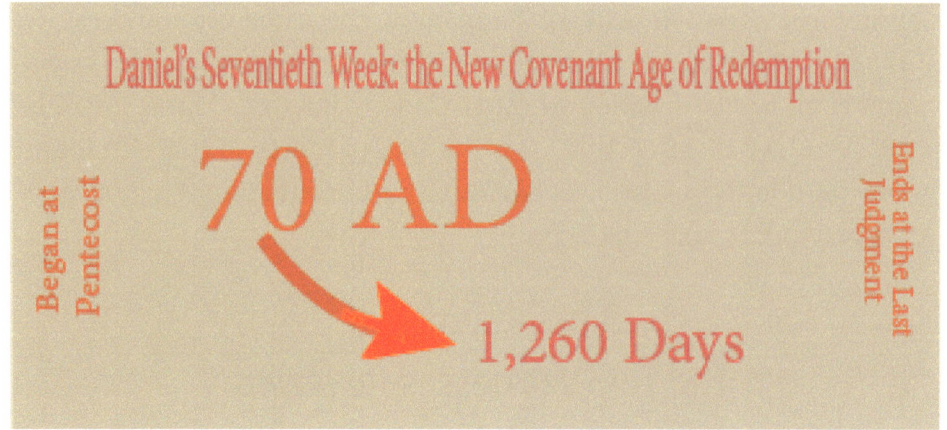

The preceding visual shows the encrypted one-thousand two-hundred sixty days, which corresponds to the second half of Daniel's seventieth week. This period is mentioned twice in the book of Revelation. The first time is in the parable of the two witnesses in Revelation 11:3, and the second is in the parable of the woman in the wilderness in Revelation 12:6. The parable of the two witnesses in Revelation chapter eleven represents the mission of the Christian church. It signifies the continuation of Christ's earthly ministry, which aims to spread the good news of God's kingdom. This mission is not limited to the first century of Christianity but extends to the future history of the church. It is also portrayed as the latter part of Daniel's seventieth week, from 70 A.D. to Christ's second coming.

The same can be said for the 1,260-day sojourn of the woman in the wilderness in Revelation chapter twelve. Please keep this in mind, as we will be dealing with the second aspect in depth a little later. But first, there is the following essential structural clarification.

CHAPTER FOUR

Introducing the Elongated Time-Transcendent Seventieth Week

It's time to clarify a common misunderstanding: the future Antichrist is not the intended covenant-maker of Daniel's seventieth week. Instead, Jesus Christ confirmed the new covenant of the Christian revelation in three powerful ways. Firstly, as a prophet, he taught the way of true righteousness during his earthly public ministry among the Jews. Secondly, as a priest, he brought true peace through the blood of his cross. And thirdly, as king, he confirmed the new covenant through his resurrection and eternal life above. It's undeniable that Jesus Christ continuously delivers on his promise to save all who come to the Father through him (Hebrews 7:25). Therefore, let's place our faith in the true covenant-maker—Jesus Christ. The Christ event of the first Christian century was a remarkable manifestation of the three-fold hope of the old covenant Israel for the coming new age of salvation bringing righteousness, peace, and joy. It was through the divine Son of God that these new age promises were powerfully fulfilled. This event is a testament to the beauty and wonder of God's plan for humanity.

To gain a better understanding of God's unique plan for human salvation, we must delve into its historical development in the Old Testament, particularly in the book of Daniel. Daniel, who lived during the sixth century B.C., records a timeline of four successive empires in the Middle East that ultimately led to the arrival of Jesus. This timeline begins with the Babylonian Empire, which was short-lived and lasted only during Daniel's lifetime. God used the Babylonian Empire to bring judgment on neighboring nations, including the Southern Kingdom of Judah, in 586 B.C. The Babylonian Captivity period is extensively mentioned in the prophecies of Isaiah, Jeremiah, and Ezekiel.

In 603 B.C., during his second year of sole reign over Babylon, Nebuchadnezzar dreamed about a colossal statue made of different metals representing the successive Gentile kingdoms (Daniel 2:28-45). Daniel interpreted these kingdoms as follows: (1) Nebuchadnezzar's Babylonian Empire (the head of gold); (2) the Media-Persian Empire of Darius the Mede and Cyrus the Great (the breast and arms of silver); (3) the Macedonian Empire of Alexander the Great (the belly and thighs of brass); and (4) the Roman Empire, which was to dominate Palestine in the New Testament era and beyond (the legs of iron and the feet part of iron and part of clay). It is said that while this colossal image still stands, the God of heaven will establish a kingdom that will never be destroyed. This kingdom will exclusively comprise God's people and will conquer and replace all preceding earthly kingdoms. Furthermore, it will last forever (Daniel 2:44).

In the dream of the great image, we witness a stone being cut without human hands from a nearby mountain. This stone then strikes the image with a powerful blow and gradually becomes a great mountain that fills the whole earth. We recognize this stone as the stone of prophecy, which is mentioned in various scriptures such as Deuteronomy 32:4, 18, 30-31, 37; II Samuel 22:2-3, 32; Psalm 31:3; 61:2; 62:7; 71:3; 118:22-23; Isaiah 28:16; 32:2; Zechariah 12:3; Matthew 21:42-44; Mark 12:10-12; Luke 20:17; Acts 4:11; Romans 9:33; I Corinthians 10:4; Ephesians 2:20-22; I Peter 2:4-8 and Revelations 4:3. This stone is none other than our Lord Jesus Christ, who was not born of natural human procreation, but is a unique individual who is fully God and fully man. He is the covenant-maker of Daniel's seventieth week.

The stone you see before you is no ordinary stone. It was cut from the side of the holy temple mount, known as Mt. Zion, in Jerusalem. Countless scriptures, including Psalm 110:2; Isaiah 2:1-5; 35:4; 51:11, 16; 56:7-8; 57:13; 59:20; 65:17-18; 66:20-22; Micah 4:1-4; Ezekiel 47:1-12; and Hebrews 12:24-26, speak of this sacred place. When Jesus ascended to the Father, he moved Mt. Zion and the holy temple site to heaven, as foretold in Zechariah 14:4, Acts 1:9-11, and Ephesians 4:8-10. Through the resurrection power of Christ, the physical artifacts of the city of Jerusalem, the throne of David, and Herod's temple were transformed into their completed spiritual realities. Today, we bear witness to the kingdom reign of Christ in heaven and the church as the new temple of God on earth. The glory of Mt. Zion is now above as the place of universal human redemption. Hold this stone in your hand, and feel its weight. Let it remind you of the holy history it represents and the spiritual transformation it symbolizes.

The ascension of Christ to the Father and his enthronement as the promised King (as prophesied in Daniel 7:13-14) marked a significant shift in the covenant economy. The old covenant's physical, local, and temporal aspects were replaced by the new covenant's spiritual, universal, and eternal benefits, as discussed in Hebrews chapters eight through ten. The Christian revelation was incomplete until Jesus was glorified and openly revealed as God's anointed. It was only after Jesus was fully exalted to his messianic kingly position of honor at the Father's right hand that the redemptive benefits of the new covenant finally became operational (Acts 2:33). The Holy Spirit was given only after Jesus was glorified (John 7:39), making the saving benefits of the new covenant universally available to all humanity (John 16:7 and Acts 2:39). Therefore, God needed to raise Christ to sit on David's throne for the establishment of the new covenant Christian age of salvation, which is now being manifested in Daniel's seventieth week.

Jesus' time on Earth was transformative for the Jewish community. He initiated the covenant, which brought many blessings to the Jews. However, his message was not limited to them alone. Jesus' resurrection and ascension marked the beginning of his universal ministry, which aimed to extend the benefits of the new covenant to all of humanity. His mission was to spread love, compassion, and forgiveness across the world, inspiring people to lead a more meaningful and fulfilling life. The legacy of Jesus still resonates today, and his impact on humanity will continue to be felt to the end of time.

The resurrection of Christ ensured the eternal continuation of his glorified personal manhood. This introduced a significant change in our understanding of time on earth. The Greek language has two distinct words for time. The first one, κronos, refers to measured time, such as days, weeks, months, and years. The second one, κairos, refers to eventful time, where time is not only measured in length but is also filled with significant events. The resurrection of Jesus Christ two-thousand years ago transformed measured time into eventful time. Since then, human history has been infused with the living Savior's presence and power.

The resurrection of the promised Messiah to the Jews marks the most significant event in the history of humankind. Time, since then, has taken on a new dimension, and cannot be measured in the same way as before. It is no longer just a mere quantity or the ordinary passage of time, but instead has transformed into event-filled time, dominated by a supernatural quality. The eternal Son of God has stepped into human experience, infusing time with new meaning and purpose. Eternal life has been imparted to us through the Spirit of the eternal Son, and time has become the stage upon which a new drama is being played out—the fulfilled time of the messianic kingdom of God on earth. As Daniel prophesied, "the stone that was cut out without hands became a great mountain and filled the whole earth" (Daniel 2:44). The resurrection of the Messiah has forever changed the course of human history, offering us the hope of eternal life and the promise of a better future.

Christ, as the covenant-maker of the entire seventieth week, owns it. Therefore, the seventieth week must follow him in the same orbit of time-transcendency that his glorified persona has taken. Jesus never stopped confirming the new covenant of redemption, and his resurrection proves it. Because he is alive, the covenant-confirming ministry continues through his direct involvement. According to the Bible, Jesus himself is doing what his Spirit does through his body, the church. This forms the theological foundation for interpreting the parable of the two witnesses in Revelation chapter eleven.

The term for weeks in Daniel's prophecy of the seventy weeks is actually sevens in Hebrew. According to *Strong's Concordance*, the word used is sheba, which has been translated by Young, following Keil and Kliefoth, to mean "an intentionally indefinite designation of a period measured by the number seven, whose chronological duration must be determined on other grounds."[1] Daniel 9:27 is saying that the Messiah confirms the covenant for one seven, which doesn't necessarily mean a literal seven years, but rather a single period of time that needs to be determined by the context. This should be our first clue that this is not a prophecy of any literal seven-year period, whether we place those seven years in the first Christian century or in relation to the second coming of Jesus Christ at the end of the age.

It is important to understand that the seventieth seven in the prophecy of Daniel 9:27 is not a literal seven-year period. Instead, the prophecy uses the word seven, making the timeline enigmatic. However, what truly matters are the events that take place. The main event of the prophecy is the confirmation of a new covenant of salvation by an ever-living Messiah for as long as the age of redemption lasts.

The one-thousand two-hundred sixty days and the time, times, and a half in Daniel and Revelation all refer to the latter half of the one seven mentioned in Daniel 9:27, which applies to the present age. Understanding this underlying structure is essential to unlocking the secrets of the Christian apocalypse. So, let's delve deeper into this now and discover the true meaning behind this prophecy.

---

[1] Young, *The Prophecy of Daniel*, p. 196.

Back to the Two Witnesses in Revelation Chapter Eleven

In Revelation chapter eleven it's important to note that the two witnesses mentioned are not human beings, but rather olive trees and candlesticks. This signifies the symbolic interpretation of the passage. The imagery of the two olive trees and two candlesticks mentioned in Revelation 11:4 is taken from Zechariah chapter four. In this chapter, God provides visions and oracles of encouragement for rebuilding the Jerusalem temple after the Israelites' return from the Babylonian captivity. Zechariah's prophecy dates back to about 520 B.C. Comparatively, in the New Testament, God's ultimate temple restoration plan is revealed to be realized through Christ's building of his church (Zechariah 6:12-13 and Matthew 16:18). Therefore, the imagery of the two witnesses prophesying for one-thousand two-hundred sixty days in Revelation 11:3 points towards the Word (symbolized by the light of the two candlesticks) and the Spirit (represented by the oil for the lights given by the two olive trees). It is increasingly evident that the prophecy about the two witnesses is now being fulfilled in the evangelistic work of the entire Christian church throughout the present age.

The passage in Revelation 11:3 that says, "I will give power unto my two witnesses," is similar to Acts 1:8, which says, "you shall receive power when the Holy Ghost comes upon you; and you shall be witnesses unto me both in Jerusalem, and in all Judea, and Samaria, and unto the uttermost part of the earth." The number two symbolizes the smallest representation of a Christian church (Matthew 18:15-20). This parable uses this number to represent the whole church. The clothing of the two witnesses in sackcloth signifies the humility and dedication of the church, and their fire-breathing and miracle-working abilities display the authority and power of the church. This is a symbolic way of stating that the church's witness to the dominion of Christ over this present age has the power to consign men to everlasting bliss or eternal damnation (Matthew 16:19; 18:18; Mark 16:16; and John 20:21-23). Christ now rules the nations with a rod of iron. That rod of iron is manifested in the inflexible degrees of the gospel that is now committed to the church to be proclaimed to every creature. The inflexibility lies in the ultimatum: "He that believeth and is baptized shall be saved, but he that believeth not shall be damned" (Mark 16:16).

In Revelation chapter eleven, the parable of the two witnesses serves as a powerful metaphor for the Christian church's mission on earth. As believers, we are called to continue Christ's new covenant-confirming ministry during the latter part of Daniel's seventieth week. This period is encrypted and transcends time, starting from the desolation of Jerusalem in 70 A.D. (Revelation 11:1-2) and culminating with Christ's second coming, marked by the last trumpet sounding of verses thirteen through nineteen. The ascension of the two witnesses to heaven in verse twelve symbolizes the church's rapture, which we believe is imminently approaching and which we eagerly await. As we fulfill our mission, we must remember the witnessing time frame of the one-thousand two-hundred sixty days. This is a critical period during which we must remain steadfast in our faith and continue to spread the good news of Christ's salvation. Let us be encouraged by this parable and strive to fulfill our mission with boldness and dedication. Together, let us eagerly anticipate the day when we will join Christ in the clouds and be forever united with him.

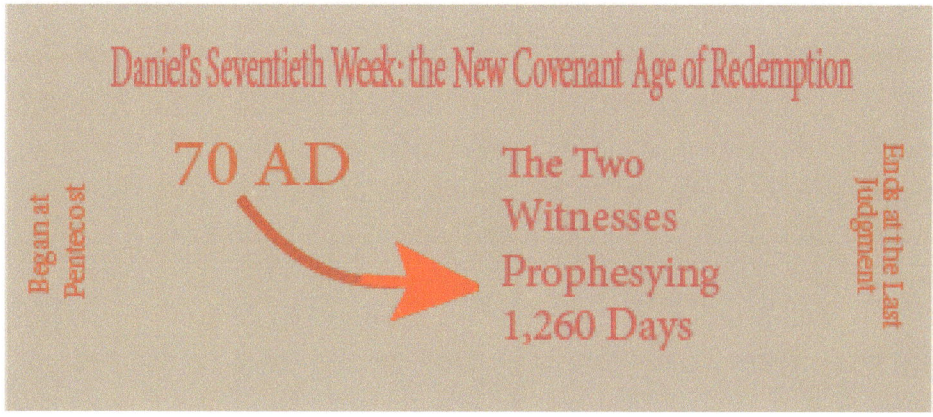

The Parable of the Woman in the Wilderness Explained

In Revelation chapter twelve, we can identify the second instance of the one-thousand two-hundred sixty day period. It appears in the parable of the woman in the wilderness. This woman is associated with Christ-rejecting Israel as the seed of the serpent mentioned in Genesis 3:15. The woman—earthly Jerusalem—is also linked to the man child, our Lord Jesus Christ (Romans 3:1-2 and 9:3-5), who was born from Israel after the flesh. After Christ's resurrection and ascension in Revelation 12:5, the woman (Israel after the flesh) flees into the wilderness of the great Gentile diaspora for one-thousand two-hundred sixty days (verse six). As we have already seen, these symbolic days refer to the latter portion of Daniel's seventieth week, representing the entire new covenant Christian age from 70 A.D. to the final judgment.

The breathtaking image of a woman in heaven in Revelation chapter twelve verse one is a powerful symbol of Israel's divine election. The twelve tribes, represented by the twelve stars, were not chosen to glorify themselves, but to fulfill a divine mission: to bring into the world the man child, the Messiah Jesus, who would change the course of history forever. This image reminds us of the profound responsibility that comes with being chosen by God and inspires us to strive for greatness in everything we do.

The third part of the stars of heaven, which were cast to the earth by the dragon, symbolizes the leaders of post-exilic Jewry who had lost their grace and were under the influence of the evil one (Zechariah 3:1-2). At the time of Jesus, these leaders had failed to protect and guide the people, resulting in their scattering (Ezekiel 34:1-31; and Matthew 10:6; 15:24). Jesus came to save these lost sheep and bring them back to the fold. However, his own people did not accept him (John 1:11-12). This was not surprising, as the veiled reference to Messiah's people who would destroy the city and sanctuary in Daniel 9:26 had accurately foretold.

As Jerusalem on earth dispersed into the Gentile diaspora, a transfer of spiritual power and authority took place in the heavens (Matthew 24:29 and Mark 13:25). Israel's patron angel, Michael, cast out Satan, along with his angels (Revelation 12:7-9). These angels were the same leaders of Israel, or the third part of the stars of heaven mentioned in verse one that the dragon had previously seduced. The dragon's power to work through backslid Israel was lost when Israel was disenfranchised from her covenants of promise and was now transferred to the Roman beast (Revelation 13:2). Israel's history had come to an end for a season, with only the fulfillment of Daniel 7:13-14, Matthew 24:30, and 26:64 left to her. However, the dragon continued to work through other means. Thus, for the next eighteen hundred years of church history, Rome would replace Israel as the seducer of the nations (Revelation 13:3-4, and 8).

In Revelation 12:14, the two wings of the great eagle symbolize Rome, which exiled the Jews to the Gentile diaspora after the catastrophic event of 70 A.D., as prophesied by Moses in Deuteronomy 28:49 and Daniel 8:23 and 11:35. Despite their dispersion in the Gentile diaspora, God preserved the Jews, all the while Jerusalem remained uninhabitable to them (Luke 24:21; Revelation 11:2; 12:6 and 14). The words desolate and desolation in Daniel 9:26-27 support this perspective as they lay bare the words of Jesus' ultimatum in Matthew 23:36-39, which directly refers to the fulfillment of Daniel's prophecy. The Jews will be restored as God's people once they are willing to call Jesus blessed (John 3:36). They will no longer be known as Jews but only as Christians (Isaiah 65:15; Matthew 8:11-12; Romans 2:28-29; 9:7-8; 10:12; and Galatians 3:26-29).

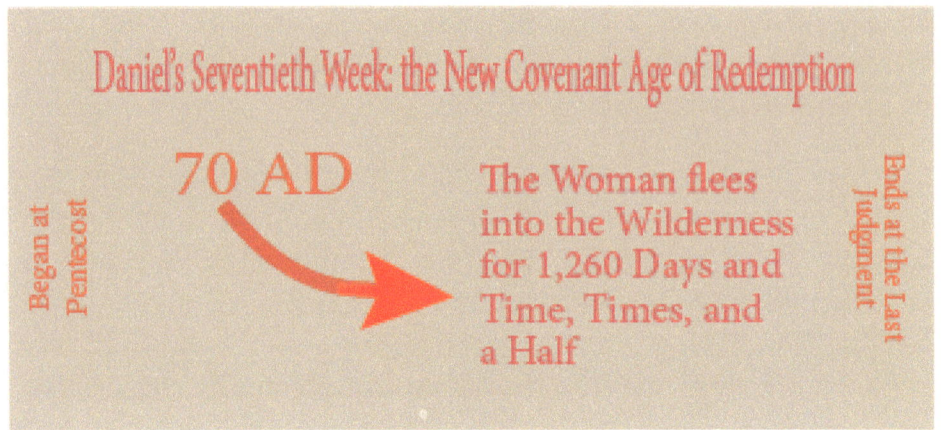

The Meaning of the Third Part Expression in the Book of Revelation

Chapter eight marks the beginning of the seven trumpet soundings, which ends with the last trumpet sounding at Revelation 11:15. It is important to note that this is when the rapture of the church and the last judgment will occur (Revelation 11:11-12, and 18). The sealed book mentioned in Revelation 5:1-5 is fully opened in Revelation 10:7-8. In chapter eight, we find a theme introduced that needs to be explained, which is the third part. This phrase is mentioned a total of fifteen times in the book: eleven times in 8:7-12, twice in 9:15-18, once in 12:4, and once again in 16:19. The background for understanding this expression comes from Ezekiel 5:12, which states that two-thirds of the Jews were to perish in the Babylonian Captivity. Among the remaining third part that would be scattered to all the winds, a remnant would return to Palestine after the Babylonian Captivity was over. The future promised to the third part of the Jewish remnant that would survive the Babylonian Captivity is amplified in Isaiah 19:24-25 and Zechariah 13:8-9.

Isaiah 19:24-25 states that in the future, Israel will be joined with Egypt and Assyria as a blessing in the land. Some believe this will happen in a post-second coming millennial age, but it is actually being fulfilled in the present Christian dispensation. The three traditional enemies of Israel, Egypt, and Assyria can now peacefully come together in the new body of Jesus Christ, the Christian church. This is possible through faith in Christ, and in him, the true blessing is found for both Jews and Gentiles. The promise of Genesis 12:1-3 is fulfilled through Christ, as he alone is the seed to whom all Israel's messianic blessings have been promised (II Corinthians 1:20 and Galatians 3:16, and 29).

The prophet Zechariah, who lived after the Babylonian Captivity, describes the future of the Jewish remnant. He says that in all the land, two-thirds of the people will die, but one-third will survive (Zechariah 13:8-9). God will refine and test this remnant as silver and gold are refined and tested. Zechariah predicts that God will sift the remaining remnant by fire, and those who endure this process will be brought into a new relationship with God as his saved people. This passage echoes what God had said in Ezekiel 5:12. According to Matthew 3:5-12, John the Baptist and Jesus Christ brought the sifting baptism of water and Holy Spirit fire. Those who were sifted into the kingdom of God by the Messiah became the start of the new Israel of God, which is the Christian church. Those who rejected the salvation of God brought to them by the Messiah were judged by him and became a desolate house (Matthew 23:37-39). They had the blood of all the righteous, including that of the Messiah himself, on their hands (Matthew 23:35-36; Isaiah 63:1-6; Revelation 14:18-20; Matthew 3:12; Revelation 19:13; and Acts 5:28).

As we delve into the expressions used in the book of Revelation, a pattern emerges. All the third-part references are directly or indirectly related to the fate of the Christ-rejecting Jews and their desolate house. A striking example is the eleven times mentions of the third part in Revelation 8:7-12, which symbolize the destruction of Jerusalem and the temple by the Romans in 70 A.D. This interpretation is not only natural but also commonsense. These first four judgment soundings leave little room for doubt. The evidence is compelling and supports the contention that the book of Revelation has a prophetic dimension that speaks to the past and the future alike.

The First Trumpet Sounding

The first trumpet sounding in Revelation 8:7 is a depiction of the loss of faith in God among the Jews who had rejected Jesus. In the Old Testament, God's people were referred to as trees of righteousness (Psalm 1:1-3). The burning up of this special relationship of old covenant Israel as trees of the Lord's planting (Isaiah 5:7) came with the judgments inflicted by the Romans in 70 A.D., just as Jesus had forewarned in Matthew 15:13. Green grass represents spiritual life—all green grass being burnt up signifies the destruction of all spiritual life. The life of God's people under the progeny of Abraham was to be a life of faith. Jesus had made it clear that if his Pharisaical adversaries had possessed the faith of Abraham, they would have recognized him as their promised Messiah (John 8:40). Those who perished in the fiery judgment of 70 A.D. had sadly lost all connection to the soul life of God through faith. Such a faithless condition towards their Messiah still remains a part of Judaism's desolate house to this present day (Matthew 21:33-44 and 23:37-39). Their division over Jesus from the beginning (John 7:43; 9:16 and 10:19) continues until now (Luke 2:34-35).

The Second Trumpet Sounding

A burning mountain can remind us of Mount Sinai, which was covered in smoke and fire when Moses received the law of commandments from Jehovah, signifying the covenant between Jehovah and Israel (Exodus 19 and Hebrews 12:18-21). The old covenant economy represented the bondwoman Hagar and her son Ishmael, who were cast out in favor of the son of promise, Isaac. So in Galatians 4:21-34, Isaac represents the new covenant heirs to the Jerusalem that is above, which is free and the mother of all true believers.

Israel was dispersed into the sea of Gentile nations during the Assyrian and Babylonian Captivities but took her religion, based on the law of Moses given at Mount Sinai, with her into the diaspora. Five centuries later Jesus the Messiah came to fulfill that law (Galatians 4:4-5), teaching that love is the fulfillment of the law (Matthew 22:37-40). During Jesus' earthly ministry, those Jews who loved God were able to respond positively to his revelation as the promised Messiah (John 8:42). Those Jews who did not love God, which the law of Moses also required (Deuteronomy 6:4-5 and Joshua 24:5), turned in animosity against the Savior (John 5:42-47 and 15:25).

The law of Moses was not an end in itself, but merely a schoolmaster to guide the Jews towards Christ according to Galatians 3:24. Once the purpose of the law covenant was served, it was done away with, cast from God in heaven back to the Jews in the sea of their dispersion. Sinai's burning mountain continued to follow the Jews of the diaspora, but it was not there to minister life, as God intended. Instead, it became a harbinger of their enduring death and damnation because they failed to keep the law or follow where it leads, as stated in John 5:45-47. Judaism, to this day, has the law of Moses but lacks true love and peace. The ships are all destroyed and are no longer suitable vessels to export the bounties of divine grace. The bloody sword has followed them, as they wished, and has become their legacy according to Matthew 27:25.

The first trumpet marked the end of faith, while the second trumpet marked the end of love. These were dire times for the Jews who had rejected Christ at his first advent. The judgment inflicted upon them can be seen in the symbolism of these trumpets. The third and fourth trumpet soundings in Revelation 8:10-12 depict the desolations wrought upon Jerusalem, signifying the end of hope. The events described in these passages serve as a warning to all who would turn away from the teachings of Christ. May we learn from history and choose a path of faith, love, and hope.

The Third and Fourth Trumpet Soundings

The Star of David is a well-known icon with occult symbolism. However, in Christian tradition, it represents hope and is associated with the wise men from the East who followed it to find the Christ child. The star of David is a symbol of hope in the promise made by God to King David about his lineage and his anointed son's kingdom. Christ fulfilled these promises by sitting on David's promised kingdom throne when he ascended to the Father. He was born, lived, ministered, died, and rose to become the king of the Jews, fulfilling the hope of David's star. This is evident in various scriptures, including Luke 1:31-33; 24:25-27; Acts 2:22-36; 13:33-34; I Peter 3:22; Revelation 4:1-3; Matthew 2:2 and John 1:49; 18:33, 39; 19:3 and 19-21.

The rejection of Jesus by the Jews of the first century was catastrophic. It extinguished David's star of hope, plunging it down from heaven as a failing torch. This star had shone brightly for a mere moment, offering a glimmer of hope that was quickly replaced by disillusionment, despair, and death wherever it fell. The rivers and fountains of waters that had once provided sustenance and hope turned bitter, leaving the Jews with no other option but Jesus (Isaiah 48:16-19 and Luke 19:41-42). Judaism without Christ has brought only bitterness and death, thereby creating a parched spiritual desert where there is no water to quench the thirsting soul. Moses had cast a tree into the bitter waters of Marah and made them sweet (Exodus 15:23-26). This tree foreshadowed the cross of Calvary, where Jesus sweetens all our heavy loads. Rejecting Jesus led to the star of David's messianic hope being dashed, growing dim, and disappearing. Without this hope, life for the Jews became a desolate house, culminating in many deaths since 70 A.D. It is time for all Jews to embrace Jesus as their savior and find spiritual life and hope.

The Fifth Trumpet Sounding

The fifth trumpet in Revelation 9:1-11 uses symbolic language to describe the opening of the bottomless pit, which unleashes five months of demonic torment on earth. This event is similar to Satan's release from the same bottomless pit to initiate the final judgment in Revelation 20:7-15. In Revelation 12:7-9, Satan is depicted as being cast down from heaven during the woman's flight into the wilderness. This event marked the beginning of the incredible Gentile Jewish diaspora after the destruction of Jerusalem by the Romans in 70 A.D. It may be helpful to pause and understand the symbolic meaning of the term bottomless pit as it is used in Revelation 9:1-2, 11; 11:7, 17:8, and chapter twenty.

The Meaning of the Bottomless Pit

Have you ever thought about what a bottomless pit really is? It's a hole with no bottom, which means that anyone who falls into it would be in a constant state of free-falling, without any foundation to stand on and unable to get their feet down on anything solid. This is the fate that awaited Satan, who has been bound by his Conqueror and consigned to the bottomless pit in Revelation chapter twenty. This powerful symbol represents the defeat of Satan and his loss of power and authority since the resurrection of Jesus Christ two-thousand years ago. It's a reminder that evil will always be conquered by good, and that we must always strive to do what is right and just.

In ancient times, the Greek word abyss referred to the unknown territory beyond the edge of the inhabited world. It was believed that the world was flat, and if someone sailed too far, they would fall off the world's edge and into the abyss. In Revelation chapter twenty, the term abyss refers to the idea that Satan has been defeated and cast into oblivion since the resurrection and ascension of Jesus Christ. This is because God has declared Jesus the Lord of all, as evidenced in Acts 2:32-36, 10:36, and Philippians 2:9-11. The idea conveyed here is that Satan's activity is not restricted, for he is still able to roam around like a roaring lion, seeking whom he may devour (I Peter 5:8-9) or like an angel of light, seeking whom he may deceive (II Corinthians 11:14). (How is it possible to incarcerate a spiritual being in a physical chain—we will talk more about this later.) However, this does not mean that Satan has legitimacy.[1] According to Matthew 28:18, John 23:31, Ephesians 1:18-23, and I Peter 3:22, Christ has made Satan subject to him. Therefore, Satan's dominion and power only exist where people allow it to be so, by failing to use the provisions of the gospel power that can bind him and cast him out.

Consider this—why would one want to distort the entirety of God's revelation just because they don't believe in complete salvation? We should understand that complete or full salvation is not only vital but also entails the binding of the strong man and spoiling his house, which is mentioned in Matthew 12:28-29. Acknowledging this crucial aspect of abundant, complete salvation (John 10:10) is essential to understand the full magnitude of God's grace and purpose, which can deliver us from all sin in this present life. Discovering the true meaning behind Satan's binding in the bottomless pit is necessary to understand the bigger picture. However, it's equally important to consider the duration of this binding, which is expressed in two symbolic terms—the forty-two months and the one-thousand years. By delving deeper into these expressions, we can gain a more profound insight into the nature of this event and its significance.

---

[1] Edgar C. Whisenant, a dispensational writer, incorrectly claimed in his controversial booklet *On Borrowed Time: 88 Reasons Why the Rapture Could be in 1988* that Satan has legal dominion over the earth until Christ returns to establish his earthly reign (p. 10). This belief reflects the typical mindset of classic Scofield Darbyism, a system of biblical interpretation heavily criticized for its failed predictions.

CHAPTER FIVE

Apocalyptic Time Frames Unsealed

The book of Revelation has been a subject of curiosity for centuries, and its prophecies have puzzled scholars and religious leaders alike. Among the most debated topics in this book are the references to a period of forty-two months in Revelation 11:2 and Revelation 13:5. Dispensationalists interpret this period as a literal three-and-a-half-year time frame, equating it with the expression one-thousand two-hundred sixty days and times, times, and a half. They also believe that the five-month period mentioned in Revelation 9:5 is a literal five months that fit into the seven-year great tribulation scenario described in Daniel 9:27. On the other hand, scholars in the historical school of prophetic interpretation believe that the three-and-a-half-year time frames may mean one-thousand two-hundred sixty years, following the day-for-a-year theory of prophetic interpretation. Regardless of which interpretation you subscribe to, and we subscribe to neither of these traditional views, it is clear that the book of Revelation contains powerful and enigmatic prophecies that continue to intrigue and inspire us. As we delve deeper into its mysteries, let us remain open-minded and willing to explore all possible interpretations, so that we may gain a greater understanding of the divine plan for humanity.

The book of Revelation uses the term month as a representation of a generation that lasts for 40 years. Several passages, including Matthew 1:1-17, Numbers 32:14, Ezekiel 4:1-8, and Joel 2:23, hint at this connection. A month is a unit of time that is measured in days, and a generation is measured in years. Just as history is progressively measured by the passage of lunar cycles called months, the passage of humans in time is progressively measured in generations. For example, Zechariah 11:8 prophesies that three shepherds would be cut off in one month, which corresponds to the casting down of the third part of the stars of heaven (the prophetic, priestly, and kingly symbols for the spiritual leadership of the natural Israel) within that generation that would experience the coming of Messiah (Revelation 12:7-9).

Daniel 8:14 is another relevant example. Here is a mysterious vision that has puzzled scholars for centuries. This chapter mentions two thousand three hundred days (literally, evening-mornings) which have been sealed up for a long time. According to the traditional interpretation of Daniel chapter eight, these sealed days started in 167 B.C., when Antiochus Epiphanes, a Syrian tyrant, desecrated the Jewish sanctuary. The phrase two thousand three hundred days refers to the evening and morning periods that were used to determine the passage of time based on moon sightings. In other words, it would take two thousand three hundred lunar cycles to pass before the sanctuary could be cleansed or properly restored. This equals one hundred ninety-one years and eight months (2,300 ÷ 12), which, when added to December 167 B.C., brings us to the year 26 A.D. This year marks the beginning of Jesus' public ministry among the Jews. *Halley's Bible Handbook*[1] places Christ's baptism as early as the Fall of 26 A.D.

During the time of Jesus' ministry, he began to restore the true temple of God on earth, the Christian church. The Old Testament Jerusalem temple, which was defiled many times by both the Jews and their enemies, is replaced by the New Testament Christian church as the eternal dwelling place of God through the Holy Spirit. Therefore, we can see that the two thousand three hundred days in Daniel 8:14 are a prophecy of the coming of Jesus and the establishment of the Christian church (Zechariah 6:12-13; I Corinthians 3:16-17; 6:19; 12:13; II Corinthians 5:1; 6:16; Ephesians 2:18-22; and Hebrews 3:6). It is a testament to the power of God and the fulfillment of his promises no matter what we face in life.

Based on the previous discussion about encryption in prophecy, we can confidently determine that the duration of the five months mentioned in Revelation 9:5, 10 represents a span of five generations

---
[1] *Halley's Bible Handbook*, p. 460.

that totals to two-hundred years. Similarly, the forty-two months mentioned in Revelation 11:2 and 13:5 signify forty-two generations that indicate a much longer duration of one-thousand six-hundred eighty years. The following diagram can help illustrate this information better.

The 42 Months	The 5 Months
of Revelation 11:2 and 13:5 are 42 generations of 40 years each or 1,680 years	of Revelation 9:5 and 10 are 5 generations of 40 years each or 200 years

The One-Thousand Years Explained

The expression commonly referred to as the millennium is a crucial topic in the book of Revelation, mentioned six times exclusively in 20:2-7. If you want to gain an in-depth understanding of this powerful concept, there's no better place to turn to than this portion of biblical literature. So, don't hesitate to delve into the depths of this fascinating subject matter.

Are you seeking to understand the true meaning behind Revelation 20:1-10? Look no further than amillennialism, the most fitting interpretation according to rational analysis. This view holds that the one-thousand years mentioned in Revelation chapter twenty is an apocalyptic symbol representing the Christian age, either wholly or partially. Both postmillennialism and amillennialism reject the premillennial theory, which suggests that the second coming of Christ happens before this one-thousand year period begins. In fact, there are ten basic arguments that prove premillennialism to be incorrect. Understanding the truth and following the correct teachings is essential to strengthen our faith and deepen our understanding of this important scripture. Choose wisely and embrace the truth today.

1. No mention of a one-thousand year reign on earth after the second coming is found in the Bible, except as some interpret Revelation 20:1-10.

2. The belief of premillennialists that Christ will only start his messianic reign after his second coming lacks evidence from Scripture. Acts 2:29-36 indicates that Christ began his messianic reign at his resurrection and ascension two-thousand years ago. Hence, he is currently reigning in his kingdom by revealing the true messianic ideal in the New Testament. To further support this, refer to Daniel 2:44; 7:13-14; Luke 1:31-33; Acts 13:33-34; I Peter 3:22; and Revelation 4:2-3. Those who believe in premillennialism are similar to the Christ-rejecting Jews of the first century who failed to understand this revelation of messianic realization taught by Jesus and his apostles.

3. There is no strong reason to believe that the events described in Revelation 20:1-10 must necessarily happen after the events of chapter nineteen in a chronological sense. It is important to note that the description of Christ riding a white horse in Revelation 19:11 is not necessarily a literal account of his second coming. According to Acts 1:11, Jesus will return to earth in the same way that he ascended to heaven. Therefore, if Christ did not ascend to heaven riding a white horse, then it is unlikely that he will return riding a literal white horse.

4. The binding of Satan in Revelation chapter twenty should not be interpreted as a physical binding using chains. Since Satan is a spiritual being, it is not possible to physically incarcerate him using physical chains. Once we accept that the chains that bind the devil are symbolic and spiritual, it becomes apparent that the woodenly literalistic premillennial argument is flawed.

5. It is important to note that if one part of the Revelation twenty passage is interpreted as spiritual, then other elements in the passage should also be considered as spiritual in nature. This interpretation does not mean that the passage is non-literal. Spiritual realities are just as real and actual as physical substances. Therefore, it is more logical to view the entire passage as spiritual rather than literal. However, premillennialists tend to equate literal with only physical or material things, ignoring that spiritual things are also literal realities. This is a metaphysical dualism that is based on ancient Platonism and does not align with biblical revelation.[1]

6. The book of Revelation is often hotly debated among Christians. Some premillennialists believe that its contents contain both literal and spiritual elements. However, this interpretation can lead to confusion and absurdity. Instead, a thorough spiritual interpretation is the only one that is logically self-consistent and makes sense. Jesus spoke in parables in the gospels, so it's not unreasonable to believe that he would do the same in the book of Revelation. The book contains parables that reveal the nature and course of this present age between Christ's first and second advents. One such parable is Revelation 20:1-10.

7. The book of Revelation indicates that the ascension of Satan, also known as the beast, from the bottomless pit in passages before chapter twenty (9:1-11, 11:7, and 17:8) should influence how the latter passage, chapter twenty, is interpreted.

8. The internal thematic evidence within the book of Revelation is crystal clear—chapter twenty recapitulates back to the first advent of Christ and carries forward to his second coming. This makes it a fitting conclusion to the main apocalyptic section of the book, providing a summary overview of events that unfold between the two comings of Christ. Just like chapter six, which expertly introduces the body of what follows, chapter twenty sets the stage for the grand finale of the book, leaving no room for doubt about the events that will unfold.

---

[1] O. Palmer Robertson, *The Christ of the Covenants* [Grand Rapids: Baker Book House, 1980], p. 214.

9. The word thousand is often used symbolically in the Bible to represent a closure on infinity, or the specifying by a term of limitation what is unlimited. For instance, Psalm 50:10 says that God owns the cattle on a thousand hills, but it doesn't mean that God doesn't own the cattle on the hill number one thousand one. It simply means that God owns everything. So, it's pointless to insist on a wooden literalism in Revelation twenty, where the thousand years most likely stands for the day of our Messiah's power, which is the New Testament's way of identifying the present gospel age. This interpretation is supported by several Bible verses, such as Psalm 2:6-7; Acts 13:22-23, 32-34; Hebrews 1:3-5; Psalm 110:1; Luke 20:41-44; Acts 2:30-36; Hebrews 1:13; 10:12-13; Daniel 7:13-14; Luke 24:51; Acts 1:10-11; Psalm 68:18; Ephesians 4:8-10; Matthew 28:18; Ephesians 1:22; Colossians 3:1; I Corinthians 15:24-28; and Hebrews 1:8, 13.

10. In his interpretation of Revelation chapter twenty, following the Lutheran scholar Alfred Bengel, John Wesley suggests two literal one-thousand-year periods before the great white throne judgment described at the end of the chapter. Likewise, in his sermon titled *The Great Assize*, Wesley believes that the great white throne judgment will coincide with the second coming of Jesus Christ. According to Revelation 12:7-10, there is evidence that supports Wesley's literal interpretation. This reference reveals that Satan was cast down from heaven (ousted from spiritual authority) between the destruction of Jerusalem in 70 A.D. and the start of the Crusades in the eleventh century, literally one-thousand years later. This binding was meant to prevent Satan from deceiving the nations any longer through the corrupting influence of Israel's wayward leadership during the long history of her checkered past. This teaching aligns with passages in the Bible such as Isaiah 52:5; Ezekiel 36:22-23; Amos 5:25-27; Malachi 1:11-12; Romans 2:24; and I Thessalonians 2:14-16.

Chapter Twenty Further Explained

Revelation chapter twenty is best understood by listening carefully to what John says he saw in the four separate visions that form the content of this chapter. These visions are not just mere observations. They are vital to understanding the chapter. Following are the four separate visions that John says he saw.

1. In John's first vision, he introduces a messenger from heaven who is of great importance and is destined to overcome the devil (20:1-3). This messenger is not just a character in the narrative but is potentially humanity's greatest benefactor. Here are some observations about this messenger: (1) He has the key, which symbolizes his authority (note 1:18; 9:1). (2) He holds a great chain in his hand, which represents the spiritual agency of gospel truth because it is impossible to bind Satan, a spiritual being, with physical chains. (3) He accomplishes his mission through five verbs: lay hold, bound, cast out, shut up, and seal. The word bound is the same as cast out in John 12:31. (4) His aim is to restrain Satan from using Israel to hinder the discipling of the nations (Matthew 28:18-20). This is not a prediction but a statement of purpose or intent in Greek, which makes a big difference. (5) His allotment is for a one-thousand-year period, which is a symbol for the duration of the messianic age that began at Pentecost and will end at the second coming when the last judgment takes place (verses 11-15). This is what we have shown in this book to be the fulfillment of Daniel's seventieth week. Jesus proves that evil angels are under bonds in Mark 3:27 and is also attested in Ephesians 1:20-22; Colossians 2:10, 15; James 4:7; I Peter 3:22; II Peter 2:4; and Jude 6.[1]

---

[1] II Peter 2:4 and Jude 6 may refer to the rebellion of Korah, Dathan, and Abiram in Numbers 16:31, or more likely to the apostasy of the patriarchal descendants of Seth before the flood. The third part of the stars, or angels cast down by the dragon in Revelation 12:4, refers back to a third of the 12 stars, or tribal leaders of Israel, in verse one. It is not based on any sound evidence that Satan was once a good angel who turned evil. Instead, the serpent in the garden was a created evil being, as were the demons who serve him (Genesis 3:1; Deuteronomy 32:39; Job 26:13; Proverbs 16:4; Isaiah 45:7; Jeremiah 18:11; and Amos 3:6). Satan was both a murderer (John 8:44) and a sinner (I John 3:8) from the beginning. Gnosticism presents a dualistic view of the origin of good and evil, while the biblical worldview is monogenistic.

2. In Revelation 20:1-6, John saw those who had suffered but were now compensated. When believers die, they go to be with Christ, who is the embodiment of the resurrection (John 11:25). In his life-giving presence, there can be no spiritual death. These souls are joined with Christ in the reign that he already experiences and has exercised since his resurrection and ascension two-thousand years ago (Daniel 7:13-14). The text does not mention that Christ establishes any kingdom on earth that focuses on the Jews or that he initiates his reign at the point of or in conjunction with the resurrection of these souls. All such ideas are mere preconceptions and conjectures. This reign of Christ is not a return to the cosmic reign that he enjoyed with the Father before his incarnation; instead, it is his true messianic kingdom reign from heaven on earth through saving grace. This reign is a current event that now fulfills the great Davidic covenant of promised blessings, as noted earlier.

3. In Revelation 20:7-11, John sees the consummation and the sovereign. He notices specific details, such as the gory battle that precedes the coming of the sovereign. Satan is the instigator of this battle, described in several biblical passages, including Ezekiel chapters thirty-eight and thirty-nine; II Thessalonians 2:1-11; Revelation 9:1-11; 11:7; 16:12-14; 17:8, and 11. John also sees the glorious brightness that announces the coming of the sovereign. Fire from heaven devours God's enemies, as described in Ezekiel 38:22, 39:6, and II Thessalonians 1:7-10. Lastly, John sees the gathering bustle as all humanity is assembled for the judgment day.

4. In the fourth vision of Revelation 20:12-15, John witnesses an intense courtroom scene. It's worth noting that this great assembly of all the dead standing before God is also described in Revelation 11:18. During the judgment, everyone is judged based on their works, which parallels Matthew 25:31-46. The scene is both gripping and thought-provoking as each person awaits to find out if their name is written in the Lamb's book of life.

CHAPTER SIX

A New Historical View of Prophecy

The opening of the six seals in the book of Revelation is a crucial event that holds great significance. However, to truly grasp the profound meaning behind it, we must first understand the background information that has been covered so far. It is only with this knowledge that we can fully appreciate the tightly woven interconnectivity between the individual details of the apocalypse. As we delve into the explanation of the seals' opening, you will begin to see the bigger picture unfold before you. Get ready to embark on an incredible journey of discovery and understanding.

The book that the Lamb opens in chapter six of Revelation is the same prophetic material that Daniel was given but was sealed up in his day (Daniel 12:5-13 and Revelation 5:1-7 and 10:1-11). From our study of Daniel, we learned that this sealed material related to the period after the taking away of the daily sacrifice and the setting up of the abomination of desolation in 12:11-12. This period refers to the last half of Daniel's seventieth week, which is the gospel age between 70 A.D. and the second coming of Christ for the final judgment. The six seals of Revelation chapter six provide us with a historical overview of the unfolding intervening gospel age. This age ends with the apocalyptic in-breaking of Christ coming for the last judgment depicted in 6:12-17.

The history of the church between the first and second comings of Christ can be divided into four distinct periods, each lasting approximately five hundred years. These periods are represented by the four horse riders seen in the opening of the first four seals of Revelation 6:1-8. The horsemen symbolize the causal dynamics that shaped and determined the destiny of each successive period. The first period began after the end of the Jewish Commonwealth in 135 A.D. and lasted until the rise of Islam in 632 A.D. The second period continued until the Crusades in the eleventh and twelfth centuries. The third period extended until the French Revolution in 1791, and the fourth period began thereafter and continues to the present.

> And I saw when the Lamb opened one of the seals, and I heard, as it were the noise of thunder, one of the four beasts saying, Come and see. And I saw, and behold a white horse: and he that sat on him had a bow; and a crown was given unto him: and he went forth conquering, and to conquer. And when he had opened the second seal, I heard the second beast say, Come and see. And there went out another horse that was red: and power was given to him that sat thereon to take peace from the earth, and that they should kill one another: and there was given unto him a great sword. And when he had opened the third seal, I heard the third beast say, Come and see. And I beheld, and lo a black horse; and he that sat on him had a pair of balances in his hand. And I heard a voice in the midst of the four beasts say, A measure of wheat for a penny, and three measures of barley for a penny; and see thou hurt not the oil and the wine. And when he had opened the fourth seal, I heard the voice of the fourth beast say, Come and see. And I looked, and behold a pale horse: and his name that sat on him was Death, and Hell followed with him. And power was given unto them over the fourth part of the earth, to kill with sword, and with hunger, and with death, and with the beasts of the earth (Revelation 6:1-8).

The First Seal
The White Horse Rider Depicting an Age of Conquest

The opening of this seal by the Lamb is being shown to the beholder, John, by the first living creature with the face of a lion. The lion-faced portion of this representation of the universal church depicts the choleric or aggressive corporate personality that manifested itself in the results-oriented evangelism done by the early church. The white horse conquering and to conquer in this vision indicates the territorial conquests that were made to advance the gospel throughout the Roman Empire in the beginning centuries of the church. The sword of the Spirit wounded that pagan beast in the hands of apostolic Christianity but later revived in the emergence of the Holy Roman Empire of the eighth century. This period of missionary territorial conquest extended from its beginning in the Jerusalem Pentecost until roughly five hundred years later at the appearance of the little horn power of Daniel chapter seven, or the rise of Islam after 632 A.D.

The Second Seal
The Red Horse Rider Depicting an Age of Conflict

The opening of this seal by the Lamb is being shown to the beholder, John, by the second living creature with the face of a calf. The calf-faced portion of this representation of the universal church depicts the sanguine or passive type of corporate personality that manifested itself in the absorption of the church with societal retrenchment and self-preservation that was characteristic of the monastic era of European church history. The red horse going forth to take peace from the earth in this vision indicates the advances of Islam that resulted in the territorial loss of Christian presence and influence in the Middle

East, North Africa, Spain, and the Balkans in the five hundred years leading up to the beginning of the Crusades. The cloistered church of this period became a drifting church, taking on doctrinal and cultural compromises that paved the way for the great spiritual darkness soon to engulf the late medieval Roman Church.

The Third Seal
The Black Horse Rider Depicting an Age of Compromise

The opening of this seal by the Lamb is being shown to the beholder, John, by the third living creature with the face of a man. The man-faced portion of this representation of the universal church depicts the phlegmatic or pragmatic type of corporate personality that manifested itself in a softened, more humanistic expression of the Christian faith, one with a heightened interest in materialism and the political dominance of the church in society. The black horse rider with the balances in his hand portrays a humanist preoccupation with this temporal life that all but snuffed out the spiritual dynamic of the church. Beginning after the Crusades, the man-centered formal Roman Church became increasingly irrelevant until it was brought to its end by the secular enlightenment of the French Revolution. By this time, Protestant reformers had recovered much of the message and mission of the church, but Christendom's lost influence in Europe was never reversed.

The Fourth Seal
The Pale Horse Rider Depicting an Age of Corruption

The opening of this seal by the Lamb is being shown to the beholder, John, by the fourth living creature with the face of an eagle. The eagle-faced portion of this representation of the universal church depicts the melancholic or aesthetic type of corporate personality that manifested itself in the diversion and fragmentation of the modern church into multitudinous aberrational pseudo-Christian sects, each with its version of original Christianity. The unity of the apostolic church was lost, and so was also the effectiveness of its evangelistic witness. Religious confusion has steadily engulfed those secular societies that have allowed such religious antinomianism or lawlessness to prevail. This era of modern spiritual devastation is reflected in the vision of the pale horse rider with death and hell following in his wake. Now Christianity for millions is just pie in the sky, completely divorced from the moral relevance that the kingdom of God came to exhibit.

More About the Church in the Book of Revelation

Dispensationalists have long claimed that the pre-tribulation rapture in Revelation 4:1-2 removes the church from the earth until the so-called revelation in chapter nineteen. However, recent studies have shown that this theory is a fanciful fairy tale with no factual basis. The truth is, instead, that the church is symbolically depicted in Revelation chapters four through twenty in numerous ways, as shown below. This portrayal of the church is diverse and conclusively proves that the church remains present on earth until the very end of time.

1. The church is pictured as the twenty-four elders in Revelation chapters four and five. These twenty-four elders symbolize the Messiah's priestly nation modeled on David's ancient system in I Chronicles chapter twenty-five. Departed souls who are now reigning with Christ in glory have received their crown of life (Revelation 2:10). The body of the old covenant people of God was not complete until it was assimilated into the new covenant church (Hebrews 11:40). The twenty-four elders represent the joining of the original twelve tribes of Israel with the original twelve apostles of the Lamb, forming one body of God's chosen people extending throughout both Old and New Testaments.

2. The book of Revelation paints a vivid picture of the church as four living creatures in Revelation 4:6-8. Unfortunately, the King James Version's translation of these creatures as "beasts" can be misleading. In reality, they symbolize a diverse new creation of saved individuals from all corners of the earth, representing all personality types: the choleric lion, the sanguine calf, the phlegmatic man, and the melancholic eagle. This imagery serves as a powerful reminder that the church is made up of individuals from all walks of life, united in their faith and their commitment to a better world. Discover the true essence of the Anointed Church through the four living creatures. They have six wings to go in any direction—forward, backward, left, right, up or down. They have eyes to see all works, and faces that mirror all walks of life. The Anointed Church embodies direction, discernment, and diversity. Let the four living creatures inspire and guide you towards a deeper understanding of the Anointed Church.

3. We have already delved into the intriguing theme of the church depicted as the two witnesses in Revelation 11:3-12. This powerful representation of the church's significance and influence deserves our ongoing attention and contemplation.

4. In Revelation chapter seven verses three to eight and chapter fourteen verses one to five, the church is pictured as the one hundred forty-four thousand sealed followers of the Lamb. The chapter begins with the statement, "Do not harm the earth until we have sealed the servants of our God on their foreheads." The word earth here does not refer to the physical elements, but rather symbolizes God's earthly people, the Jews. The harm to the Jews begins in chapter eight, where we have already discussed the first four trumpet sounds as the loss of faith, love, and hope among the Christ-rejecting Jews in the context of 70 A.D. However, before the destruction of Jerusalem took place, God had a mission to accomplish. His mission was to gather the beginning of the eternal bride of Christ, the church, from among the Jews. Jesus chose twelve disciples to build the new covenant Christian church, which would replace the twelve tribes of Jacob that had formed ancient Israel. It is worth noting that, in the old covenant Israel, not every individual from each of the twelve tribes of Jacob was sealed. Only a portion from each tribe was sealed. This suggests

that the remnant principle applies universally and completely. The number twelve represents the entire nation, indicating its universal aspect, and multiplying it by itself to the one-thousandth degree suggests the fullness of completion. The second part of chapter seven, as well as the scene depicted in 14:1-5 is a vision of the heavenly realm where the faithful believers of all nations are gathered before the throne of God. The representation of the great multitude in the book of Revelation is a powerful symbol of God's universal plan of salvation, wherein Jews and Gentiles are depicted as equals in the true remnant of Abraham's faith (Galatians 3:26-29).

These profound theological concepts of the church in Revelation chapters six through nineteen (where dispensationalists typically claim it is not to be found) encourage us to embrace our shared humanity and recognize the value of diversity in the body of Christ. This is a significant message for all believers worldwide.

The Book of Revelation as a Timeline of Jewish History

Both the Church and the non-saved Jews have figured prominently in the book of Revelation. We see the contrast very early on in Jesus' statements of Revelation 2:9 and 3:9. And that theme is further developed in the figures of the two women and the two cities as they appear in the apocalyptic symbolism of the larger narrative. First, there is earthly Jerusalem in juxtaposition to the heavenly Zion. Then there is the comparison between the faithful bride of Christ and the great whore Mystery Babylon. As the Church witnesses to the Lordship of Jesus Christ throughout this present age (chapter eleven), the woman (earthly Jerusalem) is sent fleeing into the wilderness of the great Gentile diaspora for the same duration (chapter twelve). The same woman in the same wilderness is seen as the great whore Mystery Babylon riding the eighth kingly beast, Satan, in an ill-fated attempt at world domination in Revelation 17:1-6. The scenario ends in the apocalyptic drama described in Revelation 17:16-18:24.

Here is the picture of a shocking reversal of fortunes for God's messiah-rejecting earthly people in the latter days. Its fulfillment in modern history has been seen in the rise of secular World Zionism, which now holds sway over the levers of economic and political power in much of the Roman West. This transition from the Jews being subjugated to the Roman beast at the end of the Jewish Commonwealth in 135 A.D. (Revelation chapter twelve) to their rise to dominance over the seventh American Empire beast (Revelation chapter seventeen) we have already hinted at in the previous discussion of the two beasts in chapter thirteen (see page forty-two). The forty-two months of Jerusalem's earthly subjugation to Gentile domination ended with the fall of the Holy Roman Empire during the French Revolution and the defeat of Napoleon Bonaparte, commemorated by the Treaty of Paris in 1815: the forty-two generations, each lasting forty years, total one thousand six hundred eighty years. Adding one thousand six hundred eighty years to 135 A.D. brings us to 1815 (135 + 1,680 = 1815).

An important little-known historical fact is that Napoleon Bonaparte had a Machiavellian interest in the restoration of civil liberties to the Jews, who for centuries had been crushed under the weight of medieval Europe's prevailing antisemitism.[1] In 1815 the Treaty of Paris was signed. A new day of secularization began in Europe that would increasingly marginalize the church's influence and correspondingly facilitate the dominance of the Jews in European society. These nineteenth-century societal dynamics culminated in the birth of a secular Zionist movement that paralleled the two-hundred year rise of the new American Empire that was to incorporate and supplant the dominion of Rome.

---

[1] Ben Weider, "Napoleon, and the Jews," *The Journal of the International Napoleonic Society*, Vol. 1, No. 2.

Though some contemporary conservative Christians have tried to rewrite American history to teach otherwise, the fact remains that the American beast empire was founded on the principles of the enlightenment that underlaid the French Revolution: liberty, equality, fraternity—a new secular society that would accommodate every ethnicity, every philosophical or religious tradition, and every way of life—a true cultural melting-pot as never seen before. This two-hundred-year-old political experiment in cultural relativity parallels the five-month demonic unleashing we have previously observed under the symbolism of the fifth trumpet sounding in Revelation 9:1-11.

The Treaty of Paris in 1783 marked a turning point, concluding the Revolutionary War and securing European recognition for the Thirteen Colonies as an independent nation. This moment also aligns with Revelation chapter nine's five symbolic generational months or two-hundred years. Fast-forward to 1983, a critical time during the Cold War, when we witness the United States transitioning into its role as the world's sole superpower.

From a religious standpoint, we can trace the troubling decline of early evangelical Christianity in America back to Friedrich D.E. Schleiermacher's *The Christian Faith* (1821).[1] His reinterpretation of the gospel emphasized feelings of religious dependence over the essential calls to repentance, baptism, and spiritual rebirth through the Holy Spirit. When we add two-hundred years to 1821, we arrive at 2021, suggesting the beginning of the symbolic three and a half years of the final apostasy described in Revelation 11:7-11.

This profound sequence of events warrants further exploration. In our final chapter, we will delve deeper into the biblical timeline that leads us toward Armageddon, highlighting the urgent need to reflect on our spiritual journey today.

---

[1] Earle E. Cairns, *Christianity Through the Centuries: A History of the Christian Church* [Grand Rapids; Zondervan Publishing House, revised and enlarged edition, 1981], pp. 410-411.

The Apocalyptic Fall of Mystery Babylon

The second woe pronouncement of the sixth trumpet in Revelation 9:13-19 is parallel to the outpouring of the sixth vial of wrath in 16:12-16 and is connected to the gathering of nations for the final conflict between Satan and the Lamb in 20:8-9. The Gog and Magog invasion described in Ezekiel chapters thirty-eight and thirty-nine is also a part of this narrative. Therefore, it is imperative that we read these passages together to fully understand the theme of Armageddon, the ultimate spiritual conflict. Many people misunderstand the passage of Ezekiel thirty-eight and thirty-nine, but once we grasp its true meaning, we can see its significance in the larger context of the book of Revelation.

First, we note that Gog and Magog are mentioned prominently in Ezekiel and Revelation 20:7-9. This is our first clue that this is talking about the same event. Second, the great invasion of the armies of Gog and Magog takes place upon the mountains of Israel. The mountains of Israel are those high places of spiritual revelation where God was known to dwell. "Who shall ascend unto the hill of the Lord? or who shall stand in his holy place?" and "I will lift my eyes unto the hills, from whence comes my help" are familiar expressions of this theme in the book of Psalms.

From Isaiah 2:2 and Micah 4:1-2, we learn that in the last days, "the mountain of the Lord's house shall be established in the top of the mountains, and shall be exalted above the hills, and all nations shall flow unto it." These last days are this present age in which God is now speaking to the world through his Son (Hebrews 1:1-2). As we saw earlier with the ascension of Christ, it is above the hills or in heaven itself—the heavenly kingdom throne in Zion—from where Christ now reigns on earth through saving grace. Thus, the battle described in Ezekiel thirty-eight and thirty-nine is not a literal invasion of the land of Palestine by a great army of physical horse riders from Russia, China, or anywhere else. Instead, it is the same evil forces engaged in the same spiritual warfare that we saw in Revelation 9:16; 11:7-10; 17:12-17; 19:11-21; and 20:7-9.

Notice in Ezekiel that Armageddon happens at a time when faithful Israel (the church) is dwelling in unwalled villages, a spiritual picture of carelessness and false security (38:11 and 39:6). Notice, further, that this warfare is directed against the camp of the saints and the beloved city (Revelation 20:9). Those saints are not contemporary non-Christian racial Jews that now inhabit the Zionist State of Israel. Nor is the beloved city Christ-rejecting earthly Jerusalem. Instead, this is the final onslaught of the dragon against Christ and his church. And it ends, both in Ezekiel 38:22; 39:6 and in Revelation 20:9 with the divine in-breaking of apocalyptic judgment on the dragon and his duped hordes. Fire comes down from heaven and devours them. In the Bible, there are a few instances where unburied corpses are mentioned as a symbol of the apostate church. This can be seen in Revelation 11:7-10, Ezekiel 39:11-16 and Isaiah 66:22-24. Just like in the judgment of the floodwaters, Jesus will come again to take vengeance on those who do not know God and do not obey the gospel of our Lord Jesus Christ (II Thessalonians 1:8 and 2:8).

Returning to Revelation chapter sixteen we see in more detail what is described as the final battle of Armageddon. Here comes into play what was observed earlier, which is the dramatic paradigm shift in the end-time balance of world powers—a matter that completely eludes the comprehension of modern evangelical Protestantism with its end-of-the-world Roman Antichrist system of theology. The Bible predicts, alternatively, that at the end of this final Christian dispensation, the rising power of the East will cause the apocalyptic fall of Mystery Babylon and the Roman West.

> Because of the voice of the great words which the horn spake: I beheld even till the beast was slain, and his body destroyed and given to the burning flame (Daniel 7:11).

> And the sixth angel poured out his vial upon the great river Euphrates; and the water thereof was dried up, that the way of the kings of the east might be prepared (Revelation 16:12).

The way of the Kings of the East is facilitated by the darkness that covers the seat of the beast under the preceding fifth vial of wrath out poured (Revelation 16:10). In the earthquake-like shock waves of this great political upheaval, the great city Mystery Babylon is divided into three parts (Revelation 16:19). These are:

1. Russia's challenge to the Zionist-controlled American Empire's hegemony in Europe.

2. China's challenge to the Zionist-controlled American Empire's hegemony in Asia and the Far East.

3. Islam's challenge to the Zionist-controlled American Empire's hegemony in the Middle East.

The above real-world geopolitical fissures of our present-day reflect those ancient biblical prophecies. At the same time as the rapture happens in 11:11-13, Armageddon also occurs in 16:15-21. The tenth part of the city that falls and the seven thousand that are slain in this last great earthquake denotes the end of the age of the calling of the Jewish remnant at the last judgment (Luke 21:24 and Romans 11:5, 25). The Muslim world will kill the Zionist project of the secular Zionist State of Israel once the chief sponsor of that project, the American Empire, has been neutralized. This is the nightmare scenario of every Christian Zionist. Nevertheless, this important related prophecy must not be overlooked: "when he has accomplished to scatter the power of the holy people all these things will be accomplished" (Daniel 12:7). Christian Zionists are wrong not to realize that God has made them a synagogue of Satan who say they are Jews and are not (Revelation 2:9; 3:9; and Romans 2:28-29) because Christ's first love is for his church (Ephesians 5:25-27).

CHAPTER SEVEN

The Biblical Timeline to Armageddon

The encrypted time frames of the time, times, and a half in Daniel 12:7, the one-thousand two-hundred and ninety days in Daniel 12:11, and the one-thousand three-hundred and thirty-five days in Daniel 12:12 are now being correctly deciphered for the first time in this book, and the results are compelling. They reveal that the world's end is near, and Christ will soon return for the last judgment. To those who question the promises of Christ's return, look no further. The evidence you seek is right here. Let these findings dispel your doubts and affirm your faith in the coming of Christ, just as all things had been written.

In this book, we learn that Jesus Christ, the promised Messiah of the Jews, is the divinely intended covenant maker of Daniel's seventieth week. We have also learned that Daniel's seventieth week represents the entire messianic kingdom age, from Pentecost in the first Christian century to Christ's return at the end of this age for final judgment. Here is the contiguous chronological timeline between the seventieth week's beginning and ending points.

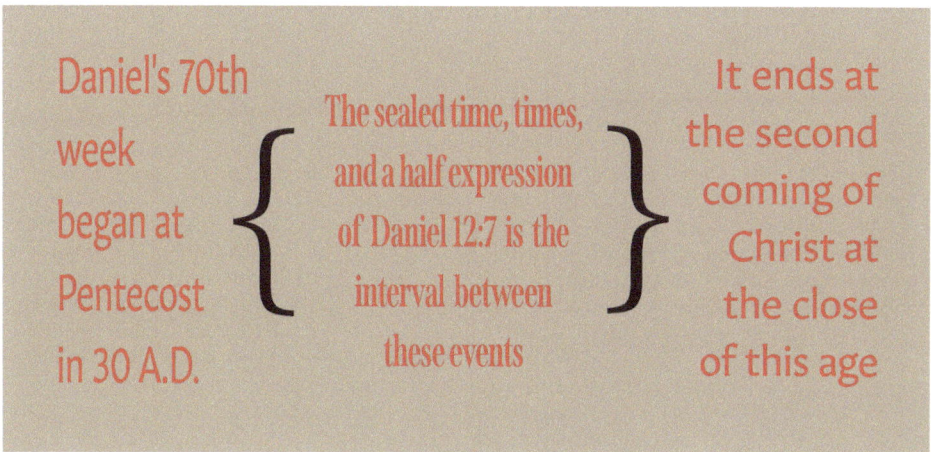

We now turn our attention to Daniel 12:4-7, a crucial passage that has already been referenced in our examination of the sealed book opened by the Lamb in Revelation chapter ten (see page seventy-three). Here Daniel is informed that the things he has witnessed in the vision that begins with chapter eleven— mostly notably the remarkable events of chapter twelve verses one through three[1]—are being placed in a book that is being sealed until the time of the end, which would occur when the power of the holy people would be scattered. That sealed duration was anonymously designated as an encryption called a time, a plurality of time, and the addition of half of a time (Daniel 12:7).

Completely bewildered, Daniel sought clarification: "O my Lord, what will be the outcome of these things?" (verse eight). He was informed that it was not for him to grasp the meaning of the symbols and was encouraged to let go of his concern (verse nine). Yet, in their parting words, the celestial messenger left Daniel with a captivating and mysterious prophecy, assuring him that the wise would eventually unravel its meaning. Now here it is, being thus unraveled.

> And from the time that the daily sacrifice shall be taken away, and the abomination that maketh desolate set up, there shall be a thousand two hundred and ninety days [which, decoded, means the first half of Daniel's seventieth week]. Blessed is he that waiteth and cometh to the one thousand three hundred and thirty-five days [which, decoded, means the end of the last half of the seventieth week] (Daniel 12:11-12).

---

[1] In Daniel 12:1, Michael standing up for the deliverance of Daniel's people, whose names are written in God's book of the faithful (Malachi 3:16-18), refers to the events recorded in Matthew 24:14-22, Mark 13:14-20, and Luke 21:20-24. The fulfillment took place during the destruction of Jerusalem and the temple by the Romans in 70 A.D. God's people that were to be delivered means Jesus' disciples. They were forewarned of the destruction and escaped to the desert fortress of Pella before the final onslaught. Secondly, we notice that the resurrection event described in Daniel 12:2 is closely linked to Matthew 27:50-53. In Daniel, the verse states: "Many who sleep in the dust of the earth shall awake to everlasting life, while others will awake to shame and everlasting contempt." Christ's death at Calvary marked a pivotal moment that led to the emptying of pre-Christian Hades, resulting in the resurrection of the first fruits, as it is noted in such passages as I Corinthians 15:2-23 and Revelation 14:4.

The First and Second Halves of the Seventieth Week Explained

The 1,290 Days of Verse Eleven

30 Days + **1,260 Days**

Additionally

The 30 days is the 'time' part of the time, times, and a half sealed formula of verse seven. It signifies a month. There are 12 months in a year. Using the day for a year theory of prophetic interpretation regarding the 1,260 days means they cover a period of 1,260 years. Using the 'time' expression as a qualifier, and dividing these years by 12, we see that the unsealed meaning is 105 years (1,260 ÷ 12 = 105), which is the real time between 30 A.D. and 135 A.D. This is also the entire real length of the first half of Daniel's seventieth week.

In apocalyptic symbolism a month is also the representation for a generational cycle of 40 years. Thus, these 30 days reveal the period between 30 A.D. and 70 A.D. or the generation that Jesus refers to in Matthew 24:34.

The 1,335 Days of Verse Twelve

| 75 Days | + | 1,260 Days |

Meaning

The 75 days consists of two 30 day periods plus a 15 day period. The repeated 30 day periods answers to the 'times' segment of the sealed formula of Daniel 12:7, while the 15 days answers to the 'half a time' segment that remains.

Additionally

The times controls how many 30 day periods there are in the 1,260 days, which is 42 (1,260 ÷ 30 = 42). As the 1,260 literal days refers to 1,260 years, so the 30 literal days refers to the parallel number of months that represent generational cycles of 40 years. So how many generational cycles are embedded in the 1,260 years or how long is the times? The answer, as we have already seen, is 42 cycles. Thus 42 generations of 40 years each is 1,680 years.

What about the remaining 'half a time'? The progressive unsealing is cumulative, as each disclosure builds on the previous one. So the half of the time refers to half of the times, or the 1,260 years. This is 630 years (1,260 ÷ 2 = 630). Six-hundred and thirty years added to 1,260 years is 1,890 years. This is the actual length of the 1,335 days of the last half of the seventieth week, which began in 135 A.D. and ends in 2025 (1,890 years + 135 A.D is 2025).

| The 42 months of the Jews in the Roman beast Empire (135 to 1815) | The 5 months of the Jews in the American beast Empire 1815 to 2015 | The end of days is the last 10 years |

The total 1,890 years of the encrypted 1,335 days of Daniel 12:12 minus the 1,680 years of the encrypted 42 months is 210 years (1890 - 1680 = 210).

A second way to view the mysterious 'time, times, and a half' expression of Daniel 12:7

The 'time' of Daniel 12:7 refers to half of the 70th week, which is the dominate 1,260 days embedded in both the 1,290 days of 12:11 and the 1,335 days of 12:12; thus we have the plural of the 'times.'

The 'half a time' of Daniel 12:7 refers to half of 1,260 days (translate years) or 630 years. 1,260 years (the time), plus 630 years (the half a time) is 1,890 years. 1,890 years from 135 A.D. (the point at which the abomination of desolation was set up) is also 2025 A.D.

A third way to view the mysterious 'time, times, and a half' expression of Daniel 12:7

'Time' is a generation of 40 years; 'times' is the 50 periods of Jewish history involved, based on the recurring 50 year cycles of the Jubilee recorded in Leviticus chapter 25. This makes a total length of 2,000 years (40 x 50 = 2,000). Two-thousand prophetic years is 1,971 solar years (2,000 x 360 = 720,000 days ÷ 365.2422 = 1,971 solar years). These years began at Pentecost (the beginning of Daniel's 70th week) in 30 A.D.

The times part of the Daniel 12:7 expression, or the 1,971 years, ended in 2001 (30 A.D. + 1,971 years = 2001*). The remaining 'half a time' of Daniel 12:7 is half a cycle of 24 years (a cycle of 50 prophetic years ÷ 2 = 24 solar years). Twenty-four years added to 2001 points to 2025 A.D. as the end of the whole 70th week and the possible coming of Christ for the last judgment fulfilling God's Old Testament Feast of Tabernacles.

WESLEYAN BIBLE PROPHECY

by Gary Cutler © 2018

TO LEARN MORE ABOUT THE BIBLICAL ALTERNATIVE TO POPULAR SCOFIELD DARBY TEACHING PLEASE GO TO

BACK TO THE LITERAL BIBLE RAPTURE: FORWARD TO THE TRUTH OF NEW TESTAMENT SALVATION

RAPTUREREVIVAL.ORG

The Times of the Gentiles Fulfilled in Secular History and in Bible Prophecy

605 B.C.	Rise of the Babylonian Empire
538 B.C.	Proclamation of Cyrus Ending the Babylonian Captivity
433 B.C.	Ezra & Nehemiah Renew the Covenant
167 B.C.	Antiochus Desecrates the Jewish Temple
5 B.C.	**Birth of Jesus Christ**
A.D. 26	Jesus Begins His Public Ministry
A.D. 30	**Calvary and Pentecost**
A.D. 70	Destruction of the Temple
A.D. 135	End of Jewish Commonwealth
A.D. 632	**The Rise of Islam**
A.D. 1070	**The Crusades Period of the Roman Church**
A.D. 1815	The Fall of the Old Holy Roman Empire & The Rise of the New Anglo-American Empire
	Rome is the First Beast of Revelation Chapter 13
	The Anglo-American Empire is the Second One
A.D. 2015	**Christ Coming in Armageddon Judgment**
A.D. 2025	**The End of the 70th Week**
	Revived Earthly Jerusalem Arising Through Secular Political World Zionism—The Woman Riding the Beast of Revelation Chapter 17

Daniel's 70th Week — The New Covenant Age of Full and Free Salvation

Daniel's First 7 Weeks Allotted for Dual Reconstruction Activity

Daniel's 62 Weeks

The Encrypted 2,300 Evenings and Mornings (Months), or 191 years, from the Temple Desecrated by Antiochus to Properly Restored Through Christ (Daniel 8:14)

The 42 Months (Generations), or 1,680 Years, of Revelation 11:2 and 13:5, Wherein Earthly Jerusalem is Trodden Down of the Roman Beast (42 x 40 = 1,680)

The 1,000 Years of the Satan's Binding, Wherein He no Longer Deceives the Nations Through Earthly Jerusalem's Corrupting Influence (Revelation 20:1-7)

The Knights Templer of the Crusades period morfed into the secret societies of Europe, such as the Illuminati and the Masonic orders. From these roots ultimately sprang the secular Christ-rejecting Western world of modern times, now deceived by the moral corruptions of the great whore Mystery Babylon. Mystery Babylon in the Book of Revelation is earthly Jerusalem, placed in glaring contrast to the heavenly Zion, where Christ now rules and reigns upon His messianic kingdom throne.

The Rise and Spread of Islam as the Historical Rival to Christianity

The "Time, Times, and a Half" of Daniel 7:25; 12:7; and Revelation 12:14 — The Encrypted Mystery of Israel's Future — The Little Horn of Daniel Chapter 7

The Encrypted Mystery of the 1,290 Days of Daniel 12:11 — An Apocalyptic Symbol for Daniel's Whole 70th Week

The Man of Lawlessness Revealed 5 generations or 200 years of Demonic Unleasing Through Humanistic Philosophies (Revelation 9:1-11)

The Encrypted Mystery of the 1,335 Days of Daniel 12:12 — An Apocalyptic Symbol for the Whole Age of the Messiah

The Encrypted Mystery of the Whole Times of Daniel's Four Gentile Beast Kingdoms Fulfilled in 2,625 Years (1290 + 1335 = 2,625)

90

CONCLUSION

Moral Realism: A Mindset Awakening

The concept of the second coming of Jesus Christ has always been shrouded in mystery and for a good reason. If people knew the exact time of Christ's return, friends of Christ would be tempted to take actions that would hasten it, while his foes would do everything in their power to prevent it from happening. Therefore, the secrecy surrounding the event's timing is necessary until the last moment to avoid any undue influence on human reactions—thus providing full latitude to human free moral agency for creating the prophesied conditions that must bring Armageddon's last judgments to pass.

The book has explored these intriguing questions, offering a thought-provoking, scholarly, compelling, and self-consistent alternative to the popular dispensational premillennial theory. It provides the flexibility of mind to see modern popular Scofield Darbyism as the facilitator of the prophesied great apostasy God has fulfilled in our modern day. With this timely truth exposure, the robust political false narrative of Western Christian Zionism is up-ended. Western Christian Zionism (based on the interpretative fallacies of nineteenth-century British premillennialism) is the principal reason for the unqualified United States support of Israel's genocide in Gaza—what looks to us like the beginning of the biblical countdown to Armageddon.

Deja vu! Could it be that God is sending us a message, and we are simply not listening? The phrase "days of Noah" implies that these events are necessary for the fulfillment of Scripture. It is the responsibility of our critics to propose a more viable fundamentalist biblical solution. With this, we confidently present our case and await the outcome, along with everyone else.

www.ingramcontent.com/pod-product-compliance
Lightning Source LLC
Chambersburg PA
CBHW040937110426
42739CB00027B/51